David C

The Emerging
High-Tech Consumer

The Emerging High-Tech Consumer

A Market Profile and Marketing Strategy Implications

Edited by
Allan C. Reddy

QUORUM BOOKS
Westport, Connecticut • London

Library of Congress Cataloging-in-Publication Data

The emerging high-tech consumer : a market profile and marketing
  strategy implications / edited by Allan C. Reddy.
     p. cm.
  Includes bibliographical references and indexes.
  ISBN 1–56720–072–9 (alk. paper)
    1. Affluent consumers. 2. High technology—Marketing.
  3. Internet (Computer network) I. Reddy, Allan C.
  HF5415.32.E527   1997
  658.8'34'08621—dc21   96–46713

British Library Cataloguing in Publication Data is available.

Library of Congress Catalog Card Number: 96–46713
ISBN: 1–56720–072–9

First published in 1997

Quorum Books, 88 Post Road West, Westport, CT 06881
An imprint of Greenwood Publishing Group, Inc.

Printed in the United States of America

The paper used in this book complies with the
Permanent Paper Standard issued by the National
Information Standards Organization (Z39.48–1984).

10 9 8 7 6 5 4 3 2 1

This book is dedicated to my parents,
the late Mr. A. Jayarami Reddy and Ms. A. Rukminiamma,
and my parents-in-law, the late Mr. CH. Sathyanarayana
and the late Mrs. CH. Balamoney.

Contents

Figures and Tables   ix

Preface   xi

Acknowledgments   xiii

1. Introduction
   Allan C. Reddy   1

2. High-Tech Consumers and Business-to-Business Markets
   Bruce D. Buskirk and Allan C. Reddy   7

3. The Internet as a Medium in Delivering Education
   Ron Barnette and Allan C. Reddy   25

4. The Telecommunications Act and the High-Tech Consumer
   James A. Muncy   43

5. The High-Tech Innovator: A Model and Scale for
   Measurement
   Jacqueline K. Eastman   55

6. Quality and the High-Tech Consumer
   Claude R. Superville and Allan C. Reddy   63

7. Global Consumers
   Niren M. Vyas and Allan C. Reddy   85

8. Distribution Considerations in Marketing to High-Tech
   Consumers
   Carol C. Bienstock   93

9. Conclusion: Marketing Strategy Implications
    Allan C. Reddy   105

Appendix A: Researching Industry Information Electronically
    Ruth Pagell   111

Appendix B: Internet Marketing
    Allan C. Reddy   123

Appendix C: Just-in-Time Retailing
    Allan C. Reddy   137

References   145

Author Index   153

Subject Index   155

About the Editor and Contributors   159

Figures and Tables

FIGURES

1.1	Considerations in Marketing to High-Tech Consumers	5
2.1	Stages of the Technology Life Cycle	11
2.2	Stage of Technology and Effort Allocation	13
2.3a	Marketing Variables through the Technology Life Cycle	18
2.3b	Marketing Variables through the Technology Life Cycle	20
4.1	A Model of the Effects of Brand Parity	50
5.1	Model of Innovativeness	57
6.1	Shewhart Control Chart	77
6.2	V-Mask CUSUM Control Chart with $d = 4.1$ and $\theta = 20.55$	78
6.3	Two-Sided CUSUM Control Chart with $K = 0.75$ and $h = 4.4$	81
6.4	EWMA Control Chart with $\lambda = 0.10$	83
8.1	Channels of Distribution for High-Tech Products	94
A.1	Extract of EIU Country Report from LEXIS/NEXIS	114
A.2	Extract of China's External Debt from DIALOG	115
A.3	Largest Computer Companies in Taiwan	118
A.4	China Company and Incorporation Profile	119
A.5	Internet Record of the CIA World Fact Book	120
B.1	Illustration of How the Internet Works	131
C.1	JIT Systems at Wal-Mart	140

TABLES

5.1   Measures of Global Innovativeness   58

6.1   Observations from an N(0,1) Distribution with a Shift of Size
      1.5 in the Mean at Observation 21   76

6.2   CUSUM Statistics with a Shift of Size 1.5 in the Mean at
      Observation 21 and $K = 0.75$ 80

6.3   EWMA Statistics with a Shift of Size 1.5 in the Mean at
      Observation 21 and $\lambda = 0.10$ 82

A.1   The World's Largest Hardware Manufacturers by Revenue,
      1993   116

Preface

Why should we study high-tech consumers? Continuous study of the changing aspects of consumers is necessary because understanding consumers is critical to the success of marketers. This book is by no means a comprehensive treatment of a complex subject like high-tech consumers; it focuses on some important issues of this emerging group. The author brings these ideas from his own research as well as through collaboration with other experts in the field.

The twenty-first century brings us instant marketing through the Internet and cable TV. Through these media we can see the emergence of a new type of consumer, the high-tech consumer. These consumers are different from those that have been familiar to marketers in the past. The new high-tech consumers are more dynamic and are interactive via the World Wide Web (WWW), cable, telephone, or satellite dishes (such as DSS or Primestar).

The profile of the new high-tech consumer is gradually evolving, with more similarities being found among global consumers than differences. One can buy new software from Australia or Canada by downloading the programs directly from the Australian sources or from mirror locations for the source available worldwide. Also, consumers can pay for their software via credit cards, which are accepted worldwide. They make the entire transaction process simple, fast, and secure.

So, manufacturers and marketers need to learn new ways to deal with these changes in the marketplace. They need to find out who these high-tech consumers are, their consumption patterns, their buying behaviors, and their brand preferences as to goods and services. If firms ignore the emergence of this new high-tech consumer, they will fall behind those who invest time and energy to know more about this new phenomenon. Thus, understanding and dealing with this new category of consumer is essential for the survival and success of to-morrow's leaders in marketing.

We usually know high-tech consumers for their high incomes, intellectual achievements, and their propensity to spend discretionary income on novel items, such as laptops and sophisticated computer programs, to make their life-style easy and more comfortable. These consumers are willing to spend good money to improve their personal productivity, and for entertainment, self-education, and job improvement.

In an age where technology is rapidly changing, the way consumers live and purchase products and services also changes, and the dynamics of these changes pose new opportunities and threats to modern marketing managers. Marketers need to properly segment the already fragile and fragmented markets, and these market segments must be effectively exploited and served to optimize corporate sales and profits. Consumers too are equally bewildered by the array of many choices they have today in each product and service category. This complicates their buying behaviors.

In a high-tech economy, marketers are concerned with how to tackle high-tech consumers. Starting with the fundamentals of high-tech consumer-buying behavior, the author enlightens readers through a series of chapters written by his colleagues, specialists on different dimensions of the high-tech consumer. The purpose of this book is therefore not only to educate the readers about the high-tech consumer and his or her profile, but also to suggest strategies that would work in marketing to these consumers.

This book is important reading for business executives of high-tech firms. It also has useful information for manufacturers and distributors and to scholars and the public who want to know what is happening in the high-tech consumer field. This book should also be of use to a variety of firms that sell their products and services through the Internet. Even mass merchandisers like Wal-Mart, de-partment stores like Sears, and category killers like Circuit City need to learn about ongoing changes in the marketplace that will affect their business in the future.

Acknowledgments

I wish to thank the following individuals for their support and chapter contributions to the book. I am grateful to Eric Valentine, Publisher of Quorum Books, for his constant support. I also wish to thank the following individuals for contributing their chapters: Ruth Pagell, Director of the Emory University Library Center for Business Information; Niren M. Vyas, Professor of Marketing and Acting Dean of the School of Business at the University of South Carolina at Aiken; Bruce D. Buskirk, Professor of Marketing and Assistant Dean of the School of Business at Pepperdine University; and from Valdosta State University, Ron Barnette, Professor and Head of the Department of Philosophy; Jacqueline K. Eastman, Assistant Professor of Marketing and Director of the MBA program; James A. Muncy, Associate Professor of Marketing; Carol C. Bienstock, Assistant Professor of Marketing; and Claude R. Superville, Assistant Professor of Management.

The Emerging
High-Tech Consumer

1

Introduction

Allan C. Reddy

This chapter introduces concepts dealing with marketing to high-tech consumers. Demographics and other marketing issues are discussed.

CONSUMERS IN THE 2000s

As we approach the year 2000, marketers need to figure out what consumers will want and how they will shop in the future. In the coming years the industrialized world will age dramatically, resulting in markets that are very different from those that exist today. As the baby-boom generation settles into middle age throughout the industrialized world, their market for consumer products will expand not only in size but also in purchasing power. The newly industrialized countries, such as Taiwan, South Korea, and Singapore, are also beginning to age. In most developing countries the population is expected to grow for all age groups, but even here a gradual aging is taking place.

A key factor in consumer markets has always been the number of women entering the work force. The increase in the number of women who work outside the home creates a demand for labor-saving devices, packaged and prepared food, and other products. Working women also typically have smaller households and greater disposable income than their stay-at-home counterparts (Czinkota and Ronkainen 1995).

Another notable population trend is the world's continuing urbanization. All told, in the future, companies can look forward to more consumers (in absolute terms) with more money to spend. And although the mature economies are aging and offer vast sales and profits to firms catering to older people, markets of products for the young and middle-aged will find plenty of market potential in the emerging industrial economies (Czinkota and Ronkainen 1995).

WHY STUDY HIGH-TECH CONSUMERS?

Consumption of high-tech products and services will continue to grow in the near future; it may reach up to 40 percent of our total purchases and consumption. Studying and understanding high-tech consumers thus is necessary to survive and succeed in business today.

Marketers are often concerned with the dynamics of changes that are happening in the marketplace today. As technology keeps growing in leaps and bounds, it affects every aspect of human life. From a marketing viewpoint, product life cycles are growing increasingly shorter, as evidenced by electronics, computers, cameras, and other products that are constantly being introduced at breakneck speeds. In electronics and computers, for example, innovations leading to constant new product introductions have become a necessity rather than a luxury. Firms that neglect to adapt to these ever-changing trends will eventually have to face extinction.

Modern consumers are also aware of the changes in the marketplace. They have access to a variety of sources that provide information about the changes that happen in the marketplace. These sources include the Internet, which keeps them informed of changes and simultaneously helps them with tools to interact with the marketplace online. High-tech consumers can now use the Internet to place orders for a variety of products and services. They can purchase new cars, electronics, computers, and software, perform bank transactions, and make travel arrangements. They can also get medical and legal assistance, do online research, and purchase and sell stocks, bonds, and mutual funds.

WHO ARE THE HIGH-TECH CONSUMERS?

A high-tech consumer is anyone who purchases and consumes innovative products and services, from general goods to electronics. A majority of high-tech products fall in the electronics category; therefore, we devote quite a bit of discussion to the marketing of these products.

We can describe high-tech consumers as middle-income, middle-aged urbanites having discretionary income to spend on high-tech consumer goods and services.

Age	18 to 65 +
Sex	Both sexes
Income	Has substantial discretionary income
Education	High school +
Location	The developed countries
Preferences	Brand loyal

High-tech consumers are generally those who purchase and consume electronic and computer novelty items associated with high technology. Though 80 percent of high-tech involves computer-related products, high-tech can prevail in many other areas. For example, high-tech is affecting education, communication, travel services, financial services, information research, and so on. Of the money that we spend each year on goods and services in the United States, how much of it goes for the purchase and consumption of high-tech products and services? We can make no accurate estimates. However, we can estimate that it is as much as several billion dollars per year.

DO HIGH-TECH CONSUMERS DIFFER FROM REGULAR CONSUMERS?

While high-tech consumers exhibit tendencies to purchase on impulse, they can also be very calculating. Therefore, firms offer these consumers free samples before they sell them the actual goods. This happens a great deal in purchasing software via the Internet. Many software companies, like Hot Dog, a HTML editor software company from Australia, believe in giving a free 30-day trial before customers decide to purchase the software. After the 30-day trial, the program may cease to work, so they compel the customer to purchase it if it is good. More software firms are trying this idea in marketing their wares. Firms use a similar approach to market to business, industrial, institutional, government, and educational markets. Another important aspect of this type of marketing is making sure that technical support is always available online. Because of the costs involved, firms are careful in offering this type of service. However, most firms offer extensive FAQ (frequently asked questions) pages that remedy most customer problems.

WHAT ARE THESE HIGH-TECH MARKETS?

Today we fragment markets more than ever, causing manufacturers to be extra careful about what they make and how they make, price, promote, and distribute their products. Excess inventory buildups can lead to losses. Therefore, producers cannot just dump excess products in the marketplace at reduced prices because that disrupts the existing channels of distribution arrangements. Frequent price changes also create an unstable image of product quality, ruining customer satisfaction, brand loyalty, and good customer relationships.

High technology is now penetrating education. Many schools and colleges have a full plethora of high-technology products and services like distance learning, teaching via e-mail, and/or web pages. Netscape and Microsoft aggressively pursue education markets by offering their web browsers free.

High-tech firms have also wooed business markets through free demos and samples. According to one estimate, online transactions will reach $7 billion by the year 2000 (*Internet User* 1996, p. 17).

Intranet marketing is a good example where a business firm with several branch offices could use customized programs throughout the organization.

Thus, they synchronize their offices with similar software and hardware. Products such as WordPerfect or Microsoft Word are now sold in combination with other software, creating integrated products such as WordPerfect Suite and Microsoft Office. These packages contain word processing, spreadsheet, database, Internet access, and other programs packed into one. Site licenses are offered; this means an organization with thousands of users has license to use the products.

Regrettably, however, cyberspace law in protecting free speech and copyrights online is frustrating. The Internet has raised legal issues ranging from copying violations to new definitions of indecency. The Communications Decency Act (CDA), passed by Congress and signed into law by President Clinton, called for fines and prison terms for individuals who distribute indecent material on the Internet. The law was never enforced because lawsuits questioned its legitimacy; it compromises the fundamental right of free speech. Thrown into the quagmire is not only U.S. law but international law as well. The United States has a broad fair use doctrine, while the policies of European countries, for example, are favorable to authors (*Internet User* 1996, p. 17).

This book examines certain important aspects of high-tech consumers, as shown in Figure 1.1. These features are presented by various contributors who are experts in their fields.

In Chapter 2, Bruce D. Buskirk and Allan C. Reddy present the concept of Technological Life Cycles (TLCs). They discuss how TLCs impact marketing strategy formulation and implementation in business-to-business markets. The TLC concept has important implications for consumer marketing as well.

In Chapter 3, Ron Barnette and Allan C. Reddy describe the Internet's impact on the delivery of modern education. The Internet is fast becoming a new medium for dispensing education. Of course, the traditional methods of classroom instruction will continue and perhaps will never be replaced.

In Chapter 4, James A. Muncy discusses the effects of the Telecommunications Act on consumer marketing.

In Chapter 5, Jacqueline K. Eastman presents a novel way of measuring high-tech innovators.

In Chapter 6, Claude R. Superville and Allan C. Reddy discuss the role of quality in high-tech product marketing. Because almost all high-tech products tend to be new and innovative, quality is very important to establish confidence in the minds of prospective consumers.

In Chapter 7, Niren M. Vyas and Allan C. Reddy discuss how the living standards and purchase and consumption habits of consumers are different in other countries. The multinational corporations marketing their products and services globally need to be aware of these changes. Ideas presented here are helpful in creating global products and services.

In Chapter 8, Carol C. Bienstock presents the structural aspects of distribution in high-tech products.

Figure 1.1
Considerations in Marketing to High-Tech Consumers

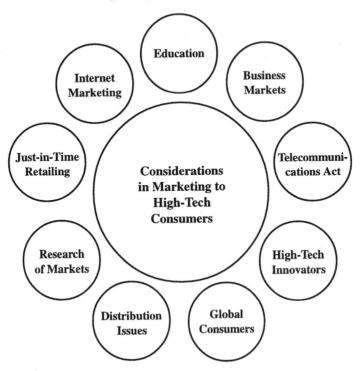

In Appendix A, Ruth Pagell presents methods of conducting marketing research electronically to find out industry information in other countries.

In Appendix B, Allan C. Reddy presents some important aspects of Internet marketing.

In Appendix C, Allan C. Reddy presents ideas about how Wal-Mart and other department stores are using Just-in-Time concepts in retailing to market products that include high-tech products as well.

WHO SHOULD READ THIS BOOK?

This book is important to policy makers and executives in public and private organizations who have a responsibility to create and market high-tech products and services. Also, it is important to scholars, researchers, and educators interested in high-tech product marketing.

CONCLUSION

This book is no remedy for all high-tech marketing problems. But it does initiate discussion of some important concepts that policy makers and marketers need to be aware of in formulating and implementing strategies for high-tech products and services.

2

High-Tech Consumers and Business-to-Business Markets

Bruce D. Buskirk and Allan C. Reddy

This chapter introduces and explores the Technology Life Cycle (TLC) concept in business-to-business markets. While we generally recognize that the marketing of high-tech products differs significantly from the marketing of traditional products, the idea that marketing must also evolve as products evolve their TLC has not been fully explored.

Industrial sales go through a life cycle, and the cycle that best correlates to these sales is the TLC. It is different from the Product Life Cycle in many critical areas. The TLC is developed and explored regarding timing and market opportunities for market segmentation.

Business or industrial markets work differently from consumer markets. Though consumer markets use the Product Life Cycle (PLC) as the cornerstone for understanding product/market behavior, the use of PLC in industrial and high-tech markets receives little attention (Ryans and Shanklin 1984). A central explanation for this difference in the applicability of PLC between consumer and industrial markets is the consumer markets' identification of technological progress.

Fashion or change for the sake of change has value to the consumer. Yet industry often fails to appreciate the drive for novelty that consumers seek. Consumers often use goods conspicuously. Goods consumed in such a manner are often believed to reflect the self-concept of the consumer. The more conspicuous the consumption, the more likely that the goods consumed will require constant fashion updating. Such conspicuously consumed goods become extensions of one's personality. For some consumer goods, fashion is the essence of the product. Therefore, fashion can be the driving factor of the consumer PLC.

Quantifying the effects of fashion changes on a consumer product versus functional improvements is difficult. Of course, the factors that decide the shape of the sales curve over time for assembly line robots are quite different from the factors that decide the pattern of the PLC for designer jeans (Buskirk 1986). On the other hand it is unreasonable to expect that the robots' sales curve would have a stable, linear growth driven only by rational, economic market processes. While both consumer and industrial factors may reflect cyclic sales, the force that drives those cycles is different.

It is therefore the contention here that the PLC is not well suited to analyze industrial markets. The PLC combines three basic trends in the marketplace: fashion, technology, and benefits sought by the marketplace. Although consumer marketing could benefit by the separation of these three factors, that is not the purpose of the discussion here. Conversely, all three factors are involved, to some extent, in industrial markets.

In industrial markets there is a tendency for customers to place much less value on fashion in the products that they purchase. Further, both consumers and industrial users are slow to seek different basic benefits than the ones they enjoyed from their adopted products in the past, unless the products' capability to provide benefits has changed dramatically. The source of change is not in the value of the benefit as much as in the ability of a product to provide that benefit. The change is in the technology underlying the product. As such, when focusing on the industrial marketplace, technology can be isolated as a critical factor causing fluctuations in sales over time in a given product category.

THE TECHNOLOGICAL LIFE CYCLE

We can divide the evolution of a technology through a marketplace, or Technological Life Cycle (TLC), into six basic phases (Reimer 1983):

1. Cutting Edge
2. State of the Art (SOTA)
3. Advanced
4. Mainstream
5. Mature
6. Decline

Although products and technologies are not synonymous, high-technology products in the industrial market are defined by and depend upon their underlying technology for their competitive advantage. Even the low-tech, well established industrial products (long considered archetypes of industrial marketing) are defined by their technologies. Low-cost production of generic goods occurs in the latter stages of the TLC. Generic products, by definition, are undifferentiated functionally from competitive offerings and are low-tech, that is, they do not provide technologically innovative solutions to the customer's problems (Popper and Buskirk 1990). Thus, these products' emphasis on efficient, low-cost production, rather than creative marketing, is simply a reflection of the technology phase dictating market segmentation strategies. Indeed, many criticisms of the PLC for consumer products, such as overlapping or indistinct stages (Dhalla and Yuseph 1976), can be resolved through application of the TLC.

Cutting Edge Stage

The Cutting Edge phase of the TLC refers to that level of technology development that is ahead of even the most sophisticated applications in the marketplace. In fact, cutting-edge technology is more research than development. To understand the role of research in the Cutting Edge phase of the TLC, it is important to distinguish between three different types of research: pure research, applied research, and product research.

Pure research seeks to find new compounds, circuits, or other phenomena never seen before. While we seek market applications for these discoveries only after the research is completed, pure research often yields easily defended patents. One measure by which firms used to distinguish the effectiveness of their pure research programs was the number of patents granted from that research. Of course, the acid test was how many of those granted patents resulted in profit-generating applications. Increased knowledge about the nature of our world and existence (the goals of pure research) does not ensure that a firm will gain a profitable advantage. In many ways, only pure research occurs in the Cutting Edge phase of the TLC.

Applied research is directed at solving an existing market problem. This style of research tends to adapt or apply existing technologies to targeted marketplace needs. The applied nature of the research goals and the existing technologies often yield hybrid technologies that do not even pass through the Cutting Edge phase of technological development.

Product research is the ongoing refinement of an existing technology. This form of research is conducted during every stage of the TLC; it serves to extend the TLC and defend the technology from newer technologies.

Cutting-edge, or leading-edge, technological firms, while principally engaging in pure research, seldom develop their technology without a specific application in mind. However, that application is likely to be limited and abstract. The measure of success for a technology is whether the marketplace can find additional applications.

There may be a target market for the pure research conducted during the Cutting Edge phase of the TLC because neither the firm nor the market yet fully understands potential applications of the technology. However, marketing efforts may be misdirected. This is not to suggest that cutting-edge firms need commercial market success to be profitable. U.S. research and development partnerships can be arranged so that the primary revenue sources of the cutting-edge firm are its tax advantages, which the firm trades to its partner(s) for cash funding (Deloitte Haskins and Sells 1982). Research grants further increase the number of otherwise successful cutting-edge firms' researches that fail to get a viable product to market.

Those cutting-edge firms that actually succeed in marketing products tend to market them to state-of-the-art (SOTA) firms that either integrate the cutting-edge product into their own product offerings or use the cutting-edge technology in discovering new market applications. These initial cutting-edge applications tend to be a combination of field testing and test marketing. This stems from the initial low reliability of cutting-edge products. In turn, this low reliability results in a high-service requirement. The high-service level represents more of a market research effort than of customer support. The wise cutting-edge firm's reaction to the problems of its service people is one technological evolution, altering and improving its products' weak points.

The firm that does not view cutting-edge technological applications as evolutionary courts disaster. The space shuttle all too vividly shows the difficulty in premature commercialization of cutting-edge technology. When errors cannot be made, progress must continue at a slower pace. One advantage of this technological evolution is that cutting-edge firms can discover unknown customer benefits and applications from observing product usage. It is at this point, when the research focus shifts to solving customer problems and responding to the market's application needs, that the TLC enters the State of the Art phase.

State of the Art Stage

State-of-the-art firms specialize in adapting developed cutting-edge technologies to market needs and applications. These SOTA firms may be cutting-edge firms that have progressed into SOTA firms through the evolution of the technology that they developed. Alternatively, they may be SOTA specialists, obtaining their technology from cutting-edge firms that wish to continue seeking new cutting-edge technologies rather than participate in the technological application of their discoveries.

As shown in Figure 2.1, marketing plays a relatively minor role in the SOTA stage of the TLC (Shanklin 1983). The markets for these products tend to be small and sophisticated. The SOTA firms tend to market the product attributes rather than user benefits because we expect that customers are able to decide how to translate the new technology's attributes into application-problem solutions (Day and Montgomery 1983). This transition away from the SOTA phase in many ways represents the end of the high-tech phases of the TLC because the firm's products are no longer technologically different from its competitors'. The death of these high-tech stages (Cutting Edge and State of the Art) is often traumatic to the firm whose self-image is intensely high-tech. Although many factors contribute to the rapid, drastic changes between the SOTA stage and the Advanced stage of the TLC, this chapter will discuss three major components: market shakeout, market share fluctuation, and market segmentation.

Figure 2.1
Stages of the Technology Life Cycle

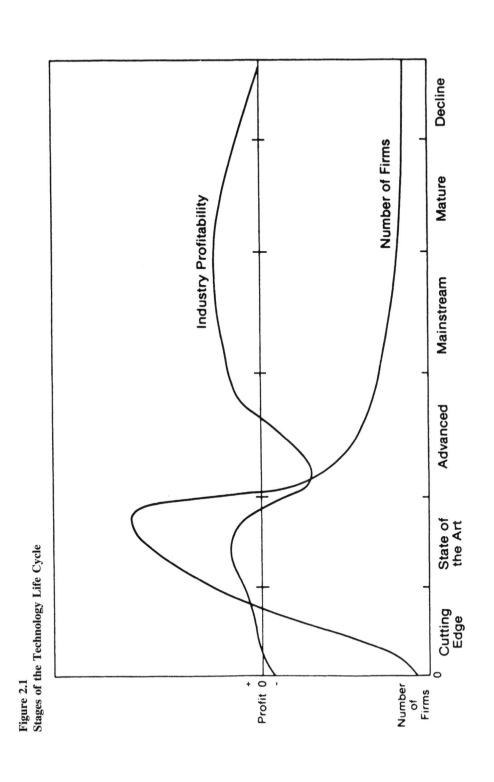

Advanced Stage and Market Shakeout

As the firm moves away from the SOTA phase, with its limited competition and sophisticated customer base, its entire operating mentality must shift if it is to continue to market its products successfully. Firms unwilling to make the necessary managerial shift should consider selling products entering the Advanced stage to firms that have the expertise required to market products in that stage.

These transition problems occur because in the first two stages of the TLC, customers are sophisticated and able to buy the products based upon their understanding of the technological attributes required to solve their problems. The same skills required to develop the product (principally engineering skills) are sufficient to market the product. With the coming of the larger market, customers are much less sophisticated but seek all the benefits they observed the SOTA firms receiving. However, these customers have no desire (and may lack the skill) to develop the expertise the SOTA firms needed to apply that evolving technology. They want bottom-line benefits, and care little about the detailed technical specifications of the product. To survive, the SOTA firm, whose product technology is maturing, must dramatically modify its competitive marketing strategy. This modification is required because the company is approaching a position in the TLC where marketing efforts are more necessary than technical (or engineering) efforts (see Figure 2.2).

One alternative available to the firm is to shift to a marketing firm. Although appearing easy on paper, such a shift is likely to be traumatic, resulting in major disruptions in the firm's management and philosophy. Frequently, this shift in orientation produces a change in top management, with the technical entrepreneurs being forced out in favor of nontechnical marketing experts. Consider, for example, the management shifts at Apple and Atari in the late 1980s.

At Apple, Stephen Jobs, one of the two computer engineers who founded the company and was largely responsible for its early growth and success, was replaced as president by John Scully, an experienced consumer marketing manager from PepsiCo. This management change reflected the different needs Apple faced as it entered an advanced stage of the TLC. In a similar move Atari brought in James J. Morgan, a senior consumer marketing executive from Philip Morris, to respond to a more aggressively competitive and dynamic marketplace unfamiliar to Atari management. Neither of these managerial shifts occurred smoothly. In both cases the firms' founders and entrepreneurial leaders left because they failed to meet the changing needs of a marketing orientation.

This transition conflict, which happens as companies move from a technical to a marketing orientation, reflects the profound differences in managerial approaches required. The nature of the relationship between technically and marketing-trained managers often lacks mutual understanding. It is this lack of understanding that so heavily contributes to the revolution in marketing orientation rather than its evolution.

Figure 2.2
Stage of Technology and Effort Allocation

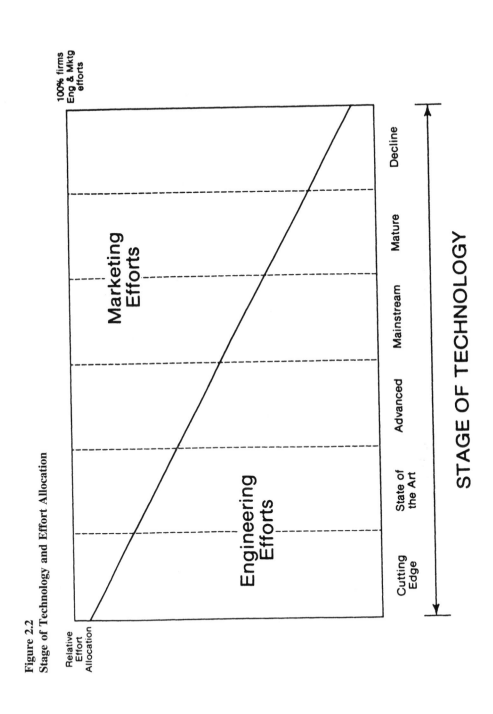

An additional complicated factor that the companies entering the Advanced stage of the TLC must face is that the potential market for high-tech products tends to be overstated (Shanklin and Ryans 1984). This is often the result of focusing on the ''newness'' of technologies and widely proclaiming the potential revolutionary impact they will have on their marketplaces. Often to their detriment, possible competitors may perceive these to be large markets. Further, the growing profit margin obtained by SOTA firms (paralleling the high profit growth during the Introductory stage of the Product Life Cycle) serves to lure competitive market entrants expectant and eager to join in the perceived huge, long-run profits. Many only hope to catch a ride on what they believe to be ''the wave of the future.''

Experience Curve Effects in the Advanced Stage of the TLC

Firms that develop a technology attempt to reap a high price for that technology while maintaining reduced costs of production due to experience curve effects that reflect both economies of scale and scope as well as learning effects (Shanklin and Ryans 1984). This can result in substantial gross margins that are usually necessary to recoup the research costs of developing the technology. These monies are also needed to fund the research and development of future technologies.

New entrants into the market are often unaware of how low the marginal and variable costs of production are, or can be, for the established developer of the technology. Make no mistake, the firm that leads on the experience curve has a natural advantage, and it is particularly difficult to catch up to the leader on that curve unless a competitor can move into the product's market share leadership position. Thus, even with ''head-on'' competition, the firm with the lowest marginal cost can flood the market with a price above its cost but below the cost of its competitors. This allows the market leader to earn profits while eliminating competition. This fact is what makes market segmentation (or niche strategies) critical to firms that cannot compete on price. While marketing can make a substantial difference, the industrial marketplace can be cruel to the best of sales organizations if their products are perceived to be inferior, overpriced, or both. This is especially true during the earlier stages of the TLC.

All these factors (managerial transition, market overestimation, and experience curve pricing) lead to a market ''shakeout,'' whereby market growth does not live up to expectation, or new entrants into the field erode market shares among market leaders. When one firm lowers price, the others must follow or risk losing a market share. Technically trained management is often too quick to turn to price reductions to solve its marketing problems—perhaps reflecting its heavy reliance on the economically based notion that all competition is based on price. Not surprisingly, as prices rapidly fall, only those firms with the lowest marginal cost survive. The industry, as a whole, often loses money trying to outlive the price war while driving their competitors out of business first and gaining large market shares for long-run profitability. In the trenches of high-tech warfare when price wars break out, the manager who attempts to cut into the competition by slashing prices is often the one who bleeds to death.

Participation in such price wars has several pitfalls. The most obvious of these is running out of money before the competition does (i.e., bleeding to death). However, there are other critical strategic considerations. For example, if product quality is lowered to support the price cuts required to compete, the customer may label the firm's products useless, thus damaging the firm's ability to "trade up" after the price war.

The price war may also train customers to be price sensitive and expect prices to fall over time rather than rise, as in the personal computer marketplace. These factors can lock a firm into the undesirable position where price is the only means of competing in the marketplace. The alternative, of course, is to segment the market and pursue a niche strategy to survive the shakeout and prosper.

Market Segmentation in the Advanced TLC Phase

The natural, and perhaps safer, alternative to price competition is market segmentation. Before the Advanced phase of the TLC, the market had not been large enough to support multiple segments. However, with the market growing in terms of units and interest, the viability of segmentation strategies is emerging. Early in the Advanced stage of the TLC, a firm is likely to lose money attempting to develop products and marketing programs designed for specific segments while simultaneously maintaining price. However, they would lose more money engaging in "head-on" price competition.

The long-term rewards of a segmentation strategy are product image, perceived expertise (both product and market), sustainable profit margin, and the ability to support product line extension and diversification after the shakeout. The basis for segmentation in the Advanced stage of the TLC can be any of the criteria typically used in business-to-business marketing (i.e., industry, product capability, channels of distribution, application, after-sale service, financing, or customer training) other than cost.

The Advanced stage of the TLC typically has a large market, often with as many consumer applications as industrial ones. This stage of the TLC best correlates to the Introductory and Growth stages of the PLC. However, the PLC does not explain the precursors to mass market entry as does the TLC.

As discussed above, firms that survive the transition into the Advanced stage of the TLC are likely to adopt a strong marketing orientation. Customers, at this point of market evolution, pressure manufacturers to standardize their products, and the marketing-oriented firms respond to their customers' needs. However, this market response varies with the size and structure of the firms.

Large firms respond to this demand standardization through product line diversification based upon product compatibility. Smaller firms push for standardization with a limited product line. Obviously, standardization is in the best interest of the smaller firms. However, it is contrary to the technological chauvinism that characterizes the cutting-edge and SOTA firms. The firms that effectively make the transition into the Advanced stage welcome standardization, while the technological specialists reject it.

If voluntary standardization is not achieved through industry agreement (reflecting the technological reservations of the SOTA firms and the successful Advanced stage firms' competitive advantage), the market will either adopt the standards of perceived market leaders (the successful Advanced stage firms) or build adaptability to different standards into their products.

Industrial firms are more demanding of standardized goods than are consumers, and they often attempt to ensure that all equipment in a given category is interchangeable. The marketing-oriented successful firms that have survived the Advanced stage shakeout may attempt to thwart what they perceive as the efforts of competitors to "piggyback" or clone their products through standardization, which results in the sharing of technology. The regulatory mechanisms control this market tension through antitrust laws that limit a market leader's ability to fight standardization, and with patents that protect the leader's technologies or its share in its competitor's profits from that technology through licensing. The advantages of such market leaders will, however, diminish, as the TLC enters the mainstream phase.

Mainstream Stage

At this stage, the market is fully developed. The technological thrust during mainstream moves from product development and application research into production research. The mainstream TLC products have achieved the standardization sought by customers, and the firm's strategic focus must shift to low-cost production. The successful firm, in this phase, is not the firm that has the most sophisticated product, but the firm that can produce the product most effectively and efficiently.

In pursuit of the Mainstream phase's production advantages, the firm may choose a capital-intensive strategy using state-of-the-art productive technologies to provide low-cost, high-quality output, with capital demands providing a barrier to entry. Alternatively, the firm may pursue a labor-intensive production strategy, which could result in moving production facilities from the country where the technology was developed to a Third World nation to reduce costs. Sometimes, this shift to offshore production may occur as early as the SOTA phase because of either a lack of capital or a lack of production-oriented technology.

Mature and Decline Stages of the TLC

The Mature technological stage is characterized by its lack of strategic production advantages. Competition shifts to customer service, as prices stabilize and the product approaches undifferentiated "commodity" status. Producers compete to establish any point of difference that could help marketing the product

Because of the lack of technological differentiation in this phase, the firm's product may be viewed as a technological commodity. The firm's technology then becomes a platform upon which other technologies are based. Simultaneously, the firm's product, while technologically mature, may still face significant growth opportunities as market applications increase. Thus, technologically mature products may not yet reach maturity in the PLC.

Finally, in the Decline stage of the TLC, other technologies displace the declined technology. The firm survives only by pricing itself substantially below the newer technology. New capital can be neither attracted nor profitably invested at this point. However, the fully depreciated older equipment allows the firm to remain price-competitive.

MARKETING VARIABLES THROUGHOUT THE TLC

Most marketing variables change throughout the Technological Life Cycle (see Figures 2.3a and 2.3b). These changes in marketing strategy and tactics vary greatly from the traditional PLC. The TLC describes multiple products based upon the same technology; this technology may move through several firms during its cycle. A PLC reflects a narrower scope.

Predicting reality, understanding it, or both is the test of a good theory. It is necessary, therefore, to evaluate the TLC against both of these tests. A common difficulty in applying theory lies in operationalizing the definitions used to identify concepts. One critical definition in operationalizing the TLC is that of *technology*. In common usage the term technology can refer to the most minute of procedures to accomplish even a very small task; as used here, however, the definition is rather broad. Unfortunately, the broader the definition of technology the less useful it is in applying the theory.

It is possible to define technology in terms of how a firm views itself. High-tech firms engaged in cutting-edge or state-of-the-art research may define technology in terms of patented discovery and will attempt to include a plethora of markets under the one umbrella. This is the correct way for them to define the technology, as no one knows what sort of market applications and benefits it may yield. However, when market application is important, the meaning of technology must shift to a definition that is based on market benefits.

An appropriate test would be to evaluate the TLC application to computers. Computer technology, when first developed, was defined by the specific functional attributes of the machines. However, this narrow application was a result of what was perceived as narrow functionality. Without a prediction of the applications that lay ahead, there was no need for a broad definition. Today there is a broadly based definition of computer technologies reflecting the wide

Figure 2.3a
Marketing Variables through the Technology Life Cycle

Stage of Life Cycle	Cutting Edge	State of the Art	Advanced
Characteristics:			
Sales	Low, mainly to state-of the art firms	Rapidly increasing as applications are demonstrated	Increasing at a decreasing rate
Costs	High, production and R&D	Unit costs high but dropping	Rapid drops with mass production, economies of scale, and learning curve
Profits	At BEP or even a loss	Rapidly rising	Huge up to price war
Customers	State-of-the-art firms	Business clear benefits or savings	Consumer markets open plus business markets

18

Competitors	Unlikely	Many upstarts, but most are technologically behind	Many new firms, food market
Objectives	Product development		
Strategies:			
Product	Demonstrated feasibility of product	Product specialization	Segmented by benefit and usage
Price	Very high, or traded for product testing assistance	High	High until possible price war
Distribution	Direct sales	Per sales network	Multi-tiered channels appear
Promotion	Personal selling principles. Some trade P.R.	Trade show presence	By distribution network

Figure 2.3b
Marketing Variables through the Technology Life Cycle

Stage of Life Cycle	Mainstream	Mature	Decline
Characteristics:			
Sales	Peak and may start to fall	Props as substitute technologies emerge; saturation	Decline
Costs	May go offshore if not already offshore	Level	Level, but cheaper technologies exist
Profits	Profits recover from shakeout; eliminate competition	Harvesting	Minimal
Customers	Broadest base	Innovators find newer technologies	Laggards

Competitors	Oligopoly	Oligopoly	Newer technology
Objectives			
Strategies:			
Product	Product standardization	Share too minimal	Obsolete
Price	Traditional pricing	Traditional pricing	To meet new technology
Distribution	Less service; less price distinction	Distributions start to fall with sales	Limited
Promotion	Increases due to brand competition	Price-based sales; sales promotion	Little

and increasing range of computer applications, including assembly line robotics, mainframes, minicomputers, and personal computers.

Where just a few years ago we touted the computer as infeasible, today the technology has already progressed through the Cutting Edge and State of the Art stages. The market shakeout has occurred and the drive to standardization characteristic of the Advanced stage of the TLC is ongoing. Computer technology rigidly conformed to the TLC's predictions.

A related example is the digital wristwatch, which that is actually an unsophisticated calculator, which, in itself, is a simplified computer. (Indeed, the Casio wristwatch calculators have as much computing power as the early vacuum tube computers.) The watch prices, which started at $300, fell to $5 in less than two years. The producer of the low-cost product was Texas Instruments, known for its engineering orientation. Using experience curve pricing strategies, TI dropped the price of the watch to single digits by using a plastic case and taking advantage of its accumulated experience in manufacturing integrated circuits. Watches, once characterized as expensive, fashionable, and a major purchase, became an impulse item or a novelty. TI believed it would dominate the watch market by giving the world a low-cost, functional watch free of the demands of fashion; however, it destroyed the total market size. Many consumers preferred to go without a watch rather than sport a cheap, unfashionable piece of plastic.

It is also important to note that not all technologies move through the entire TLC. Some life cycles are trimmed as the existing technology is supplanted by a new and superior technology. One example of this technological truncation was the replacement of mechanical adding machines by electronic calculators in the 1970s. Other technologies are only slightly diminished. Today people ride bicycles and trains, drive automobiles, and fly subsonic and supersonic jets. When the new transportation technologies entered the market, the then dominant technology evolved into a focus strategy with its own target segment. Each of the new technological innovations expanded the total demand for transportation without eliminating the existing technology. Indeed, some older technologies (bicycles, for example) are stronger markets than they were before the arrival of the new technologies.

Market segmentation and a firm's stage in the TLC are intertwined. Firms whose existence was established by engineers, and whose niche has been maintained through technological superiority, should not continue selling products based upon widespread maturing technologies. This is the realm of marketing-oriented firms. History has shown that firms experience great difficulty in maintaining excellence in both engineering and marketing. Engineering-oriented firms need to sell or ''spin off'' their aging technology and concentrate on developing new technologies. This is their segment.

For the purpose of short-term planning, we can define technologies quite narrowly. New technology seldom has significant impact overnight. Thus, the question is, What new technologies are going to find applications in the market-place?

Long-term planning must define technology in a scope broad enough to include other technologies that are expected to affect the market. For example, marketers of computers must realize that what we now view as "computer technology" and "electronic communications technology" may merge.

CONCLUSION

New high-tech firms must decide their focus early. On one hand, companies can attempt to follow their technology through its life cycle, adapting to the needs of each stage. Alternatively, companies may wish to specialize in a particular stage of technology and continually develop new products to replace those that progress to later stages of the TLC. The firm that decides to follow its products through the TLC needs to evaluate its capabilities at each stage and grow with the product. The firm that wishes to stay in the same stage of technology must know when it is time to sell its technologies.

The traditional Product Life Cycle does not help high-tech firms address these real market problems. However, following the Technological Life Cycle, planners would examine the potential impact of new technologies as they develop. Market reaction, or overreaction, to new technologies can be evaluated for their long-term effects. Industrial marketers should heed Levitt's advice in "Marketing Myopia" (1960); their industry should be defined in terms of benefits rather than products.

The Technological Life Cycle provides a mechanism for product segmentation for term-market planners. For long-term planners, the TLC serves as a tool and a road map for strategic planning.

3

The Internet as a Medium in Delivering Education

Ron Barnette and Allan C. Reddy

This chapter explores how modern technology, such as the Internet, is used in delivering education. It further provides examples of how some distance-learning courses are taught. Electronic delivery of instruction to remote sites, known as distance education, offers opportunities for students at subsidiary campuses to take classes that are not often available at their location. For the Internet, there are no boundaries; American teachers can educate people in remote China or India if they have access to the Internet.

Dr. Ron Barnette, head of the philosophy department at Valdosta State University (VSU), offers a philosophy course via the Internet using electronic mail (e-mail). He also developed an award-winning home page that can be reached on the Internet. It has extensive information and valuable links to a variety of sources of information (see http://www.valdosta.peachnet.edu/~rbarnette/phi). Apparently, students that enroll for the course at VSU get the full credit of five quarter hours. However, it is not clear how non-VSU students claim credit from their own institutions for this course. Important aspects regarding this type of distance learning include speed, convenience, and the availability of the instructor. The material is posted on the Internet on a 24-hour basis, and tests are conducted via e-mail.

Dr. Barnette also teaches other distance-learning courses, and VSU offers courses through interactive television to students living in nearby communities. Students go to nearby colleges that employ television monitors; they hear live lectures and talk with the instructor through television conferences.

Through distance learning, an instructor can offer his or her course to hundreds of off-campus students. Furthermore, because of its practical cost, distance learning is widely used in China to educate the masses.

One great disadvantage of distance learning, however, is the inability of the student and instructor to interact with each other face to face. Interaction that takes place through a television conference is not synonymous with classroom learning.

USING E-MAIL AS AN INSTRUCTIONAL AID

Electronic mail (e-mail) is a kind of computer-mediated communication that allows for both one-to-one and one-to-many interactions via a host or mainframe computer network. Most e-mail systems, for example, the PINE system, support such services as distribution lists, group addresses, and departmental networks. Very similar to online bulletin boards, these systems allow any message or article posted to be automatically received by all those included in the list.

Thus, anyone receiving messages can either "read-only" or add their own messages. Software is now also available for some e-mail systems whereby users can compose messages offline. This has at least three advantages: it greatly reduces the time online and may decrease long-distance charges; it frees up the telephone for other uses; and, most important, it allows users to take advantage of word-processing software products, which are usually more convenient to use than word editors supported by e-mail systems. Therefore, in this presentation, the term *e-mail* is used to cover all the functions discussed above, namely, one-to-one, two-way communication, distribution lists or bulletin boards, and offline editing.

How useful is e-mail to teachers and students? E-mail's most important feature is its capacity to create a close connection between teacher and learner or among groups of participants at the time and pace of their choosing. Also significant, it can provide an electronic environment very similar to that of computer conferencing. Although less sophisticated than computer-conferencing systems, e-mail systems allow us to do many things that only computer conferencing used to provide. Let's compare this with some key features of computer conferencing summarized by Mason (1994, p. 50).

Electronic mail to one or more individuals on the system; conferences in which a set of participants can read and write a group of messages; subconferences within conferences so that different topics of discussion can be distinguished. Therefore, in the following section, some examples are drawn from my experience with distance courses in which computer conferencing was the mode of delivery. These useful activities are now also feasible with e-mail systems, provided some arrangements are made with mainframe computer services.

What Has Been and Can Be Done with E-mail Technology?

In this section I will briefly summarize the instructional activities that have been or can be carried out via an e-mail system. Of course, this list is very limited to my experiences and imagination; therefore, readers are cordially invited to add to it. Basically, there are five categories of activities that can be accomplished with the e-mail system:

1. Online Material Presentation. In this category, e-mail is used to present relevant course materials prepared for discussions. If scanning facilities are available, lengthy documents or reading materials can also be presented with ease. Learners can submit their assignments or electronic journals through e-mail and share them with the class if appropriate.

2. Online Collaborative and Project Work. This basically means that if two or more learners decide to take up a group project, the e-mail system is a very convenient way for students to send work back and forth. They receive feedback before submitting their work to the instructor or presenting it to the whole class.

3. Online Help Hotline. Requests for assistance can be directed to either the teacher, teaching assistant, or the group, thus drawing on collective wisdom. Sometimes, e-mail also enables people to find help outside the class community. In any course, inviting a guest speaker to contribute up-to-date information and valuable experience and to answer challenging questions would be helpful. With the conventional classroom approach, usually experts are invited to the campus. This involves much work of a logistic nature, such as finding an appropriate guest who is available; handling details concerning date, time, pay, and parking; and other material preparations. In addition, enough time must be allocated for the guest to deliver the information and for the class to have the chance to raise issues, ask questions, or debate points made by the guest. As long as the guest we would like to invite has access to e-mail, he or she could be invited to either speak to the class or join the ongoing discussion. This would not only eliminate the logistic problems mentioned earlier but also facilitate the interaction between guests and participants.

4. Online Group Discussion. As mentioned earlier, small group activities or group discussions are often very time-consuming, thus preventing participants from having equal ''air time.'' With e-mail, unfinished discussions can be continued.

Further, group discussions can be conducted that give students access to a virtual space which supports extended discussions. Participants have as much ''air time'' as they need without infringing on the rights of other students (Lauzon 1990). Online group discussions can also be carried out in various other ways, such as role playing.

For this, I would like to mention two examples. First, the online role playing was achieved successfully through a small conference in a graduate course I took via computer-mediated communication. The subject of the course was educational evaluation: alternative approaches and practices. As part of the course activities, participants ''registered'' for the conference on educational evaluation approaches under the names of famous scholars. The participants wrote contributions toward the discussion from the perspective of the roles they adopted. The intentions of this simulation were to further compare and analyze the characteristics, strengths, and limitations of a variety of concepts covered in the course materials and to see how certain issues would be handled when different approaches were applied. The instructor, acting as mediator, first set the stage and atmosphere by introducing who's who, the theme of the conference, a keynote speaker, and so forth. Presentations and discussions followed. There were also similar socializing functions to the conferences, except that they were verbally participating, of course.

With e-mail, accounts under the role name could be obtained by making arrangements with mainframe computer services. Alternatively, the instructor or the mediator could have participants send messages to his or her e-mail account first and then forward the messages to the distribution list after changing the students' names to those of the roles they adopted.

The second example was role playing that used the thinking hat framework invented by Dr. Edward de Bono. (White hat: An objective look at data and information; Red hat: Legitimizes feelings, hunches, and intuition; Black hat: Logical negative, judgment, and caution; Yellow hat: Logical positive, feasibility, and benefits; Green hat: New ideas and creative thinking; Blue hat: Control of the thinking process. For details, please refer to his Six Thinking Hats.)

The thinking hats involved participants in a type of mental role playing. At any moment a learner might choose to put on one of the hats or might be asked to wear or remove a hat. All participants could use a hat of a particular color for a few moments at a time. We used this method when we discussed a controversial perspective with regard to teaching. The whole class was first requested to wear the White hat and try to identify the major issues, concepts, assumptions, beliefs, intentions, and actions concerning this perspective. Then the whole class was divided into four or five small groups, with each group choosing one of the hats to look at this perspective on teaching from different points of view. The result was a very constructive discussion. The method may seem extremely simple, but it did work.

It may be obvious that these two kinds of role playing can also be applied successfully in face-to-face teaching situations. However, the practices would take so much time that it would be very difficult for all the students to participate. Therefore, we could not possibly afford to utilize them without neglecting other important activities.

5. Evaluation. There are many ways to measure the success of a course. Usually, a standard evaluation form is handed out near the end of the course, asking participants to reflect on their experiences. The problem with this kind of routine evaluation is that obtaining thoughtful responses amid the rush of end-of-course activities is hard. On the other hand, students appreciate timely feedback from the instructor. With e-mail, formative evaluations in the form of feedback or a questionnaire could be used. If anonymity is needed, this could be achieved through a mediator. In addition, as electronic journals, assignments, and online discussions are likely stored in the e-mail home directory or downloaded, they could be easily retrieved for self-evaluation by students. As well, midterm or final examinations can be conducted online.

What Are the Advantages?

In his *Technology, Open Learning and Distance Education*, Tony Bates (1995, p. 207) has summarized the instructional benefits of computer-mediated communications (including e-mail) as follows (and I personally concur):

Develops academic discourse

Provides collaborative and project work

Builds knowledge

Maximizes the knowledge and experience of all participants

Increases equity of participation

Provides cross-cultural participation

Helps develop reflective writing skills

Decreases social isolation

Offers emotional involvement

Offers ready access to help and support

Provides feedback to and direct student contact with the central academic team

Offers active and interactive participation

Provides the freedom from constraints of time and location

Offers learners control (For details, please refer to the book itself)

In addition, e-mail technology is relatively cheap and simple to use. With menu-driven configurations becoming prevalent, the systems are quite user-friendly. I would like to quote Linda Harasim: "At issue is . . . how to build upon and retain the complexity of an environment like computer conferencing so that users learn to be critical thinkers by considering issues and ideas from many perspectives" (1990, p. 59).

Although student engagement and the quality of discussions—two crucial aspects in improving our teaching—would be greatly improved with e-mail, they could prove very challenging tasks in terms of writing. For one thing, apprehension concerning how one's writing might be interpreted by readers could deter a person from using the keyboard. Therefore, turning online group discussions into online role playing might help people overcome this barrier.

What Are the Disadvantages?

The use of e-mail as an aid in classroom instruction could also lead to some undesirable effects. For example, at this stage, e-mail is still a limited symbolic representation system void of oratory and graphic appeals. Primarily textual, it is very demanding on our writing abilities, to avoid misunderstanding. One student in the class commented that one has to "be explicitly clear about humorous comments, jokes.'' Also, to assume all learners would prefer writing to speaking is not warranted. Some students expressed their frustration about lengthy time spent going through messages and typing responses, when orally, the exchanges could be done in just a few minutes. For people who like to stare at the screen for lengthy periods, much more paper is likely to be consumed downloading files.

Using e-mail as an instructional aid is also limited to certain kinds of learning. For the learning that requires demonstration, e-mail in its current phase cannot replace such an experiential learning event. Although online discussions could achieve the same dynamics as that of buzz groups or the richness and stimulation of face-to-face encounters, they may form a new dispositional barrier toward participation, namely, computer anxiety or computerphobia. In one course, when a writer proposed using e-mail for journal writing, it was vehemently denounced by many learners who obviously had negative experiences with computers.

Cost and access are still major barriers as well, especially when computing services in some schools are transformed into cost-recovery enterprises. Many learners at some universities have to rely on the school terminals rather than on personal computers to get free e-mail services. Thus, their freedom in choosing the time and place to be online is restrained.

Advantages and Disadvantages of Using E-mail for Instruction

This is an excerpt from Xin Li's presentation, which includes some practical ideas on how e-mail technology has been and can be used to aid classroom instruction.

Three major types of education are possible: (1) courses delivered through computer-mediated communications; (2) courses that use computer-mediated communications as part of course activities; and (3) courses in which no computer use is required. This presentation is an integrated reflection on all the three modes of instruction.

CONCLUSION

In short, the use of e-mail for classroom-based instructions has many potential advantages. They are potential because the positive effects will likely be outweighed by the undesirable effects if caution is not exercised against disadvantages that might occur. After all, computers are tools, and the instructor who decides whether to employ e-mail technology should ask himself or herself a very important question: What am I trying to accomplish with my teaching? However, as discussed in the book *Distance Education and the Mainstream*, there are indications that teaching methods used in distance education and in mainstream on-campus education at the postsecondary level are beginning to converge. (Smith et al. 1991). Integration of e-mail technology into classroom teaching might be such an indication. As Tony Bates (1995, p. 202) pointed out:

It is still open to debate whether this technology will result in truly new paradigms, or merely allow valued old paradigms to be used more effectively for learners. Nevertheless, there is a great deal of innovation in the use of computer-mediated communication in education, and it is also one of the fastest growing technologies, in terms of the numbers of teachers and learners who are using it.

Therefore, development in this aspect is well worth our attention and further exploration.

EXPERIENTIAL INFORMATION FROM PRACTICAL VIEWS OF PEOPLE TEACHING DISTANCE LEARNING

Ron Barnette, "Reflections on Electronic Frontiers in Education"

As a concerned educator, I constantly seek ways to improve my teaching and learning effectiveness. In this respect, I am an experimenter. We must undertake educational experiments, however, with sensitivity and care and implement them with a clear and thoughtful direction in mind. Otherwise, one's professional integrity and ethical responsibility to students could be compromised. Therefore, the inevitable question becomes, Just how much can we deviate from traditional educational techniques and methods?

With this question in mind, I contemplated offering a Special Topics in Philosophy course during the summer quarter of 1994, to be conducted totally through the electronic medium. Using the Internet, how would a class in which members know one another only through their written thoughts differ from the standard context wherein bodily presence is an integral part of communication and class discussion? There would be no body language for cues, no predisposed attitudes based on race, gender, or age—just each other's ideas to go on, including my own, as crafted in text and exchanged for debate and critical discussion.

How would library research projects fare in this medium, where online resources available through an electronic source would constitute the only research infrastructure instead of physical trips to the library? Where individual critiques would be prepared and essays shared among authors whose personal identities and attributes are shaped mainly by what one writes and expresses? How, indeed, would cyber classmates develop relationships with one another and with me? How would I fare in this virtual educational community, where disembodied ideas reign?

After discussions with colleagues and students, I decided to develop and conduct such a course. Titled "A Virtual Classroom: the Electronic Agora," the course was accessible online twenty-four hours a day, seven days a week, for the eight-week quarter. Twenty-one members made up the class, with eight taking the course for university credit. Most participants were university students, with one in Texas; one in New York; one in Illinois; and one in North Carolina, in addition to the remaining on-campus Georgia members. Several Valdosta State faculty members were active as well. During the 1995 summer term, PHICYBER II was offered, building on the original course outcomes; its successor, PHICYBER III, was taught in the summer of 1996. An interactive web site was launched to facilitate all course activities, and a Virtual Library was established, containing links to some 3000 complete, searchable works. Zeno's Coffeehouse offered online puzzles and problem-solving activities. One hundred eleven participants from eleven nations and five continents enrolled in PHICYBER III, which enabled ongoing multicultural exchanges to be supported in a lively manner. (The web site's address is http://www.valdosta.peachnet.edu/~rbarnette/phi)

Two main activities that address the central objectives of a philosophy course are research and class discussion with critical dialogue. Through Valdosta State University's Philosophy Internet Gopher service, a Virtual Library was created containing more than one hundred philosophical texts. Course handouts were posted as well, and all resources could be fully searchable electronically. These resources have grown tremendously and are now featured as the international Philosophy Subject Tree by the American Philosophical Association, available to scholars worldwide. Geographical limitations for library visitors suddenly vanished, substituted by cyberspace accessibility that transcended these spatial and temporal inconveniences. Further, there was no cost for classroom materials, at least in the traditional sense.

All classroom discussions and dialogues were conducted through e-mail, via PHICYBER (Philosophers in Cyberspace), an electronic list to which class members subscribed. (The list continues to serve as a forum and electronic marketplace [hence Agora] for classroom exchanges.) It was remarkable to watch interpersonal relationships unfold. Members responded to the discussion topic, defended their positions, objected, responded to challenges, and reflected on implied new directions for analysis and further critical thought. As one student put it, "It is so different when we have to think through our ideas, put them in writing, and be prepared to back up our views, knowing that once expressed they are out there for the permanent record!" Indeed, all classroom work and discussions were placed in a course archive and made available for ongoing retrieval and review. Think of the course as a transcript. There were no voices or accents, no noises, no people—only ideas and ideas on ideas, formulated, written and rewritten, expressed, and resisted.

During the final two days of the quarter, those who could physically arrange it met together for the first time to discuss their experiences. They watched, listened, and talked to each other, in part to identify in human form those participants whose identities were formed by thoughts alone! It was plain that compared to the classroom setting, this Electronic Agora was the real market-place of ideas, where thoughts seemed to take on a life of their own, and we thinkers were but vehicles for their transmission and replication. And now, face to face, we had the business of physical metamorphosis to contemplate.

The original experiment was too good to abandon; after a piece describing it appeared in the *Chronicle of Higher Education*, I received many inquiries, which helped shape plans for PHICYBER II (the 1995 summer version). Global in scope, the second Electronic Agora involved participants from some nine countries who explored multicultural themes in this multicultural marketplace. The dynamics were fascinating to examine, especially in light of computer-mediated worldwide communication and collaboration. The web site provided additional benefits over the previous summer, particularly in the multimedia area. Whether one climbs aboard as a full-credit student or as a cyberauditor, the electronic voyage should be quite an odyssey. As an aside, there are current deliberations concerning cyber-tuition costs for future "cyberversity" attendees.

To wrap up: I am convinced that the electronic medium can provide unlimited opportunities, as long as those opportunities are seized by responsible, mature participants. Example: disabled students whose creative ideas and abilities can be enhanced without the encumbrances of unfortunate spatial and temporal logistic problems, or those whose physical arrangements might otherwise preclude engagement in university scholarship and dialogue. I am equally convinced that the Virtual Classroom model should be a supplement to existing university life. I am old-fashioned and wise enough to realize that face-to-face interactions are indispensable educationally. After all, these occasions shape real-world involvement.

Responsible choices and alternatives in the new electronic frontier should be made only upon thoughtful, reflective balance; given that, electronic education experiments can bring out the best of what diversity in quality education has to offer.

Daniel Peraya and Claus Haessig, "Designing Teaching Material for Distance Education: The Case of the Fernuniversitaet and the Open Universiteit: A Comparison between Two European Distance Universities"

From 1990 to 1993, in the European program TEMSUS (TransEuropean Mobility Scheme for University Studies), Switzerland participated in the Fernstudienzentrum Budapest Project (abbreviated as FSZ Budapest), whose objective was the creation of a distance-teaching center in Budapest. The Fernstudienzentrum Budapest was inaugurated in 1991 and now has more than 150 students. They can follow courses in economics, electronics, mathematics, computer science, environmental protection, social sciences, pedagogy, agronomy, and modern languages. The courses are taught in German at the FernUniversitaet of

Hagen, Germany (henceforth FU) and in part in English at the Open Universiteit of Heerlen, Netherlands (henceforth OU).

Swiss participation was placed in the hands of two university centers with different objectives. The first, initially attached to Zurich University—then to Basel—is mainly preoccupied with the intercultural problematics that necessarily arise in a trans-European collaboration. It has, moreover, become involved in the training program for tutors. The second work group, composed of members of TECFA (Unit for Learning and Training Technologies) of the Faculty of Psychology and Education Sciences of Geneva University, has been entrusted since 1991 with a comparative study of the methodologies of creation of training material furnished to FSZ Budapest by FU and OU.

We have analyzed the specific characteristics of the teaching material produced and used by both universities in a threefold procedure: a comparative inventory related to the principles of structuring the teaching materials, a presentation of design methods, and finally a description of existing design practices.

The design methodologies and the production procedures for teaching material differ considerably between the institutions. It is no doubt that the FU formulated the more coherent theoretical model for methodology. It is based on the interaction of the three components of distance teaching: the subject matter, the media, and the learner. During the design of the teaching material, their respective roles are shared by four actors: (1) the teacher/author, a central pivot of the subject matter elaboration process; (2) the expert in media didactics; (3) the expert in didactics of the subject as specialist of instructional mediation; and (4) the analyst who considers the learner's needs.

The OU has chosen a more pragmatic, therefore, less formalized, methodology and approach. It allows for a taxonomy of the media comparable to that of the FU; however, its methodology is inspired less by an interactionist model than by a series of extrinsic criteria that are divided into three groups:

1. market criteria, such as cost-effectiveness and scale economies;

2. exploitation criteria, referring to distribution, examination ease, the needs for practical work; and

3. tutoring criteria, touching on ease of use, the possibility of insertion into a technological context, and the life expectancy of the technologies.

We stated at the beginning of this text that all production of distance-teaching materials—traditional printed material, interactive software, communication technology, and so forth—requires a strictly defined pedagogical outlook and methodology. This is indeed the case for the universities studied. However, the methodologies set up do not follow only the criteria of their respective outlook or pedagogical bias. They are at least, if not more so, modeled on institutional data and constraints. The role of the teacher, which greatly determines the processes of production of the material, is a characteristic example. Conceptual models and institutional models, therefore, seem to condition each other to push the practices in a direction that the pedagogical criteria do not entirely govern.

Rory McGreal, "Report of the Subcommittee of the Advisory Board of the New Brunswick Distance Education Network on Choosing an Audiographic Teleconferencing System"

(Note: This material is abstracted from a report compiled as part of a course in computer technology in education taught by Dr. Marlyn Kemper-Littman of Nova Southeastern University.)

This subcommittee was constituted to evaluate audiographic systems and choose the best one to meet the needs of the network in New Brunswick. After an initial survey, two systems were judged competent: The Optel Telewriter (TW) and Vis a Vis (VV). Both are DOS-based systems, although a Windows beta version of TW was demonstrated. VV informed us that they are developing a Windows version. These systems were examined at demonstrations given by the vendors in March 1993. Subsequently, another system that uses Windows, Smart2000 (S2), was tested.

The evaluators noticed no significant differences in the following features:

ability to transmit data and voice

ability to scan images

flexibility in importing graphic images

ability to print visuals

capacity for multipoint teleconferencing

potential for upgrading software

ability of vendor to deliver quickly

upgradability to two-way compressed video

There were notable differences in the following features:

Ease of Use. All three systems were easy to use. The TW differed from the other systems in that the features were accessed by pointing to squares on the tablet; the others had icons on the screen. There was a preference expressed by committee members for the onscreen icons, but it was felt that the VV icon area took up excessive screen space. The S2 icons took up very little room at the bottom of the screen. They could also be moved around and positioned anywhere on the screen.

Functions. The VV had a fully functional system in place. The S2 was a beta version for multipoint teleconferencing. The TW Windows version was demonstrated but not made available, so most testing was done on the DOS version.

Vendor Support. Talco (TW) in Canada is a small Canadian branch of a larger American company with no representation in the Maritimes. Smart2000 (S2) and Worldlinx (VV) are larger companies in Canada with an effective customer support system. In addition, VV has a representative with ADCOM in Saint John and others in Halifax; VV's demonstration illustrated this high level of support.

Customer Base. TW is widely used in Canada. Newfoundland (Tetra), Northern Ontario (Contact North), and other provinces have extensive systems. TWs are also widely used in the United States, Australia, and parts of Europe. VV is used in many parts of Canada, the United States, and Finland. It is significant to us that a VV data bridge is being used in Nova Scotia, where they seem committed to VV. Generally, S2 is not widely used; however, Microsoft uses it for training and communication purposes.

Blackboard. All three units were remarkably easy to use. All the testers preferred the S2. An annoying feature of both the S2 and VV systems was the default white background.

Cost of Tablet. The small S2 Acecad tablet was considerably lower in price than those of the other companies. Both VV and TW used summapads. (S2 can also operate with a summapad.) VV and S2 systems can also operate with a mouse, but this is not recommended.

Remote Screen. The TW had a clear text directory that was easy to operate. The VV's slides had low-quality micro-images, while the S2's showed good-quality micro-images with a title.

Screen Capture. The S2 is the only system that is Windows compatible. The TW Windows version had not yet been beta tested when it was demonstrated. This gave the S2 a clear advantage. Users could capture screens from other software without leaving a program. In addition, the S2 file sorter was superior to the others.

Video Image Capture. The S2 has the advantage of Windows and the file sorter.

Cost. The tenders were confidential, but the lowest price came from the S2 vendors. It was much lower than the VV and considerably lower than the TW.

Compatibility. Compatibility with the other provinces in our region is important to us. Unfortunately, the two other provinces with systems are split between TW in Newfoundland and VV in Nova Scotia. New Brunswick already has eleven TW systems that we can use for receiving courses from Newfoundland. We felt that if Nova Scotia institutions wanted to deliver to some of our sites using VV, we could purchase a few software packages for that purpose.

Bridge Cost. The TW and S2 systems are comparable in price for a 32-port bridging system. The VV system was more expensive.

MAC Compatible. Many of our institutions, especially the secondary schools, use MAC computers. It is important for us to have some compatibility with them. The VV has a MAC version. The TW has no plans for a MAC version. The S2 is developing a MAC version that is promised for the Fall of 1993.

Windows. S2 is a Windows program. TW has a beta version of its Windows software. VV is developing a Windows version.

Shared Applications. Of the three systems, S2 is the only one that supports sharing of real time-running Windows software. Programs like WP for Windows, Autocad, and others can be shared over multiple sites. Annotations can also be made over the running programs.

Training and Manual. S2 had an easy-to-use manual, and it was prepared to offer training on demand. TW expected more money for training and for extra manuals. VV and TW manuals were more difficult to read.

Robert A. Oehlkers, "Interactive Television Survey: Summary of A Survey of Distance Education Interactive Television Users"

Hardware

The hardware used was made by VTEL, PictureTel, Compression Labs (CLI), and NEC. A number of users commented on the easy-to-use VTEL and PictureTel hardware, mentioning that they were reliable as well. No one mentioned hardware difficulties; however, line connections and training were problematic. More on this later.

Compression

Almost all responses showed that some form of compression was used. The popular rates mentioned were 768K and 384K. Although 56K for conferencing was also mentioned, such quotes as "slight jerkiness when viewing, but students get used to it after 20 minutes"; "first bothered by a 128K image"; and "can live with it" were typical.

One commented that the compressed video was flexible in that more sites could be tied together, whereas the full motion video was limited to four sites.

Audio

Quite a few felt that audio was more important than video. Such quotes as "If audio is not clear, all is lost"; "The video is seductive, but far too much time is wasted on video quality, when it's the audio that supports true conversation"; and "This is the #1 issue of concern because it is often taken for granted. Believe me, don't ignore audio" were indicators that audio consistency is a vital problem.

Classroom Design

A few indicated that camera placements produced problematic classroom design. Users are working to better the design, but it is a trial-and-error process.

Support Personnel

Two respondents indicated that a technical person was required at each site. They felt this relieved the instructor of the technical burden and was a major factor in the success. One respondent had difficulties and commented, "At the corporate level, nobody seems to know how it operates"; as a result, "I'm getting used to teaching on the radio" (with his Interactive Television System).

The second respondent was a coordinator who could bridge between the user and the technical expert. She said, "I found the technology relatively 'easy' and the inter-institutional cooperation/coordination the hard part." To me, this is clear: a team of technical support person, coordinator, and instructor is a requirement, not an option.

Other

One person mentioned using the Internet and such systems as CU See Me, Show Me, and MBONE. No one indicated they were using these for distance education instruction. Typically, the use was based around conference needs. My personal belief is that we will see more Internet use as people adapt to the technology. This is an area of great potential, and its time will come; we just have to catch up.

Takeshi Utsumi, "One-to-Many Multimedia Broadcasting System for the Third World"

Introduction

Improving and expanding education are essential ingredients of any national development policy. Countries look to the future's well-educated generations to improve their overall social and economic standing. Because of the economic advantages, electronic distance education has been perceived as a powerful means to use telecommunication technology for the dissemination of teaching experiences and ideas; for access to and sharing of information; for the production of two-way exchanges; and for bridging time and space limitations.

This project proposes that an integrated systems approach to the development of an electronic distance education system for remote areas be economically undertaken in phases to provide effective, affordable, and timely delivery. It further proposes that state-of-the-art industry equipment and resources can be used to reduce exposure to failure, to maximize use of existing resources, and to allow developments to add to the whole rather than render it obsolete. It requires minimum invention yet promotes innovation within time and economic constraints.

The project would entail collecting data, providing a test platform, reporting on developments, producing working systems, and deploying a reasonable solution for ubiquitous access to necessary resources. The project would be set up in three phases to allow gradual costs to be developed; to allow time for support funding to be raised; and to reduce the complexity of study and planning by using small working systems that can be scaled up to global deployment. Phase One would use emerging systems to test, study, and develop initial teaching techniques. Phase Two would deploy working sites for testing and development of training systems and keep up with emerging technology. Phase Three would provide operational systems using the defined and perfected systems from Phases One and Two, including the one-to-many system.

By using a variety of electronic techniques, all participants can communicate but at different bandwidths or speeds. By studying what works now and defining the parameters to build access to the global community that is affordable for all, this project strives for integration and equality of electronic exchange beyond broadcast television, circuit-connected telephony or computer networks.

Global contact can be achieved at an affordable price. Whether by outrigger or space shuttle, the information explorers of the twenty-first century can be anyone from anywhere.

"Multimedia of America (MMOA)" Project

Global (electronic) University (GU) (a divisional activity of Global Systems Analysis and Simulation Association in the United States [GLOSAS/USA]) is now soliciting participants from Third World countries who may be interested in a joint project of developing a one-to-many, receive-only multimedia system that could be deployed at an affordable price; it would be simple to operate and maintain and would work on standard communications and computer systems. The system would allow transmission of voice, color video, and data over an inexpensive voice grade channel. Videos of an instructor; handwriting in color on an electronic white board; images and graphics with annotation; and dynamic graphic presentations by real-time execution of an application program, simulation model, and so forth can be seen in windows on the receiver's computer screen.

The resulting system will be a "Multimedia of America (MMOA)"—analogous to the shortwave receiver for "Voice of America." Students at participating schools can receive an American education with the one-to-many broadcasting system, containing high levels of interaction and feedback (via electronic conferencing) among students and instructors. In the near future, students in any remote location can receive courses from America (later from any other country), and they can earn degrees from Global University. Teachers and professors (active or retired) can transmit their courses from their offices or homes through ordinary telephone lines for worldwide broadcasting, for example, via packet-satellites. This system will be developed in the Third World countries by using land lines, existing satellites, and earth stations.

Global University

The Global (electronic) University (GU) consortium seeks to improve the quality and availability of international educational exchange through telecommunication and information technologies. Another goal of GU is to empower Third World citizens, by giving them access to the educational excellence available from all over the world. Students could absorb a far greater variety of philosophies, courses, and instructional styles than they ever could on a single campus. This is the twenty-first-century version of the Fulbright exchange program.

Over the past two decades GLOSAS/USA has played a major role in making possible the extension of U.S. data communication networks to other countries, particularly to Japan, and in deregulating Japanese telecommunication policies for e-mail. GLOSAS/USA has also conducted many "Global Lecture Hall™" (GLH) videoconferences by employing inexpensive media accessible to the less developed countries.

These demonstrations have helped build a network of leaders in the electronic distance education movement. International associates of GLOSAS/USA are currently working on the establishment of Global Pacific University (GPU), Global Latin American University (GLAU), and Global European University (GEU).

GLOSAS/USA is currently establishing an electronic distance education system (EDES) for Russia with the Association of International Education (AIE), which was established by the Ministry of Science, Higher Education, and Technology Policy of the Russian Federation, GLOSAS/USA, and a Global University in Ukraine (GU/UKR). GU/USA has already gained wide support from prominent educational institutions as well as from information technology and industry specialists. GLOSAS/USA has also received inquiries and proposals from many countries, making this an international project to help ex-communist countries. Once in place, EDES will later become the Russian Electronic University, a part of the Global University system, as will GU/UKR.

Global University is an evolutionary concept with no precedent. GU attempts to provide cooperative, experiential learning opportunities on the widest possible scale to foster peace and sustainable development. This is the right time for global education. Technology is now available. What we need now are people who are eager to face the challenges of our time and to forge ahead toward twenty-first-century education. Interested parties should contact Dr. Takeshi Utsumi of GLOSAS/USA.

Leo A. Lucas, "NII-Based Education and Training Project"

Background

This section describes the NII-Based Education and Training Project, a joint effort among AimTech Corporation; The Consortium on Financing Higher Education; Digital Learning Services; Enterprise Computing Institute; and Oxford Academy in response to a Technology Reinvestment Project (TRP) grant administered by the Advanced Research Projects Agency (ARPA) and the National Science Foundation (NSF).

Strong educational and training systems are essential to the prosperity of our nation. As a country we invest heavily in education and training: $261 billion for primary and secondary education, $164 billion for higher education, and $43 billion for corporate training. Despite this investment, we still have significant obstacles to overcome.

Purpose

The goal of the NII-Based Education and Training Project is to use the National Information Infrastructure (NII) to fundamentally change the economics of the education and training marketplace for the benefit of all participants. Despite the best efforts of educators, trainers, publishers, and educational institutions, it is too difficult and expensive to create a completely customizable learning environment for all citizens with the current technology. We will use technology to enable educators and trainers to build high-value learning modules that can be integrated into programs that meet all the needs of our citizens. Access to these learning programs is possible anytime, from any location, and through any affiliation of the learner—by using the NII as a delivery vehicle.

At the heart of the NII initiative is the widespread adoption of computers and networks by industries, schools, and governments. The Internet and other private networks are successfully delivering electronic mail and increasingly sophisticated information servers. We will build on these successful network technologies to enable a NII-based educational and training marketplace, by creating tools that allow educators and trainers to develop and deliver learning modules. These tools will take advantage of the unique properties of worldwide network delivery, by incorporating a rich linking mechanism that tags learning modules with additional information about the content, use, and access rights of the module. The use of this new technology will lower the cost of producing, publishing, and delivering training and education. The lowered costs will fuel a competitive marketplace that will increase the availability, diversity, and quality of training and education. We will begin to communicate the value of this technology by building sample applications and tools that show its effectiveness.

Participants

AimTech Corporation. AimTech Corporation develops and markets cross-platform software tools for developing sophisticated, interactive multimedia applications.

The Consortium on Financing Higher Education (COFHE). The Consortium on Financing Higher Education is an institutionally supported organization of 32 colleges and universities. A not-for-profit coalition of universities that track and influence factors affecting the business structures and processes of higher education, COFHE provides guidance and recommendations concerning the tools, the interfaces for the educational modules, the course content, the royalty mechanisms, and the publishing policies throughout this project.

Digital Learning Services (DLS). For more than 30 years, Digital Learning Services has offered high-quality technical training and educational services to its customers. As one of the top technical training companies in the world,

Digital Learning Services provides a broad range of open, multivendor training courses, consulting services, and custom solutions.

The Enterprise Computing Institute (ECI). The Enterprise Computing Institute is a private not-for-profit research center. The Institute conducts research and development programs aimed at advancing state-of-the-art technology in computing, communications, and education.

Oxford Academy. Oxford Academy is a private, elementary day school that accepts children for kindergarten through eighth grade.

Project Outline

The NII-Based Education and Training Project will produce and deliver tools, technology, and sample applications designed for immediate use by the educational and training community. Every effort will be made for rapid distribution of the knowledge and the experience gained from this project to encourage the broadest possible adoption. Our tools will focus on the Internet because it represents the most successful network in the world. These products could further be adapted to additional network delivery vehicles, as proposed by the NII.

Technical Approach

The primary thrust of the project will be to utilize existing protocols and standards available for worldwide network applications. The training modules will consist of a very large range of popular and standard media formats. The authoring system allows for several media formats to be added.

CONCLUSION

Although distance-learning alternatives have unique advantages, classroom learning will not be replaced. Student-to-student and student-to-instructor relationships are vital for effective learning. Distance learning, therefore, can be viewed as a beneficial supplement rather than a core educational medium. Educational institutions that use distance learning properly to augment their existing curriculum and to serve their students need to be commended.

4

The Telecommunications Act and the High-Tech Consumer

James A. Muncy

This chapter presents implications of the Telecommunications Act for high-tech consumers and high-tech markets. Most of what we now think of as high-tech is either part of, or integrally related to, the telecommunications industry. Cellular phones, fax machines, the Internet, any new advance in television or sound transmission, picture imaging and transmission, satellite transmission and reception, modern location identification devices, and so forth are either the very tools of the telecommunications industry or depend on the telecommunications industry for their existence. Therefore, when changes occur in the telecommunications industry, companies interested in high-tech marketing need to stand up and take notice.

Possibly the biggest event in the telecommunications industry in the last 60 years happened on February 8, 1996, when President Bill Clinton signed Public Law 104–104, better known as the Telecommunications Act of 1996 (TCA). Though this law is very new, and it is too early to pinpoint all the ways it may impact on our lives, it is certainly not too early to look at the ways this act may impact on those who sell high-tech products.

First, this article places the TCA in its proper historical perspective. Second, it discusses the specific provisions of the act. Third, the chapter discusses how the TCA is likely to impact on various high-tech industries over the next few years. Finally, the chapter discusses many important marketing implications of the TCA. It is hoped that with the overview of the TCA as presented in the current chapter, those interested in the marketing of high-tech products can react successfully and take advantage of many changes that will likely occur over the next few months and years.

A HISTORICAL PERSPECTIVE ON THE TCA

At 11:34 A.M. on February 8, 1996, in the halls of the Library of Congress, President Clinton grasped a pen that President Eisenhower used almost forty years earlier to sign the Interstate Highway Act. With this pen, he signed the Telecommunications Act of 1996 into law. The interstate highway system brought Americans closer together physically, and it allowed the United States to maintain its leadership role in the world economy.

Nevertheless, a country needs more than highways to provide an adequate infrastructure to face competition from around the world. It needs the ability to distribute massive amounts of information instantaneously. It can fully manage and use the various means for transmitting voice, images, sounds, and so forth to almost every home, business, school, and hospital in this nation.

By its very nature, however, the telecommunications industry presents a whole host of unique problems. These problems stem from dealing with communications across distances. Only two feasible options exist for broadcasting communications across such distances. One is to string wires across people's property. Most people, however, would not permit such lines to be strung across their property unless the government forces them to do so. How best, then, to manage the lines that, for the most part, have been strung by order of the government?

The other option is to transmit communications through the air across specific wavelengths. For order to reign, however, some fair and equitable way to allocate and use such airwaves needs to be employed. Until the recent passage of the TCA, the major legislation regulating the telecommunications industry was the Communications Act of 1934. Naturally, a lot has happened in the last 62 years to require new rules dictating how this industry is to operate. Thus, we have the Telecommunications Act of 1996. Congress debated for decades on how best to update our telecommunications laws. Finally, in early 1996 Congress passed the TCA.

Most people view the TCA as fair and are optimistic about its effect on the industry (Rockwell 1996). However, some are concerned. As so eloquently stated by Bernstein (1996), "Despite the hoopla, the new telecom reform act has a reasonable probability of becoming the new seating plan for the deck chairs on the Titanic. Those with 'position' have been granted better views. However, when the ship hits the iceberg, those near the lifeboats will survive" (p. 21). It should also be noted that there is some skepticism concerning whether the Federal Communications Commission (FCC) has the resources to accomplish everything it is expected to, according to the TCA's terms (Buerger 1996; Pappalardo 1996).

Due to the unique nature of the telecommunications industry, most economists once believed that much of it was a "natural monopoly." As such, government regulations rather than the free market has been the major force determining what occurred in the industry. However, that began to crumble in 1984, when Judge Harold Greene implemented the Modified Final Judgment (MFJ), resulting in the dissemination of telecommunications giant AT&T. AT&T retained the long-distance portion of the industry, and several regional holding companies (RHCs) were formed to handle local service.

These RHCs, or Baby Bells as they are sometimes called, continued as virtual monopolies in the local exchanges, while AT&T ventured into the new world of competition on the long-distance side of the business. AT&T was barred from competing in the local exchange markets, and the RHCs were prohibited from competing in the long-distance markets. Before long, the RHCs wanted a chance to compete in the lucrative long-distance markets, and AT&T wanted its share of the local markets.

Eventually, Congress decided that if competition could be instigated in the long-distance markets, then perhaps it could also be developed in other aspects of the telecommunications industry, such as cable television. The idea led to the TCA, a 106-page document that covers everything from coordinating interconnectivity to controlling the transmission of violent and obscene material. Though a full legal discussion of all aspects of this bill is beyond the scope of this chapter, the major sections are explored below.

AN OVERVIEW OF THE TCA

Reed Hundt, Chair of the Federal Communications Commission, delivered a speech at the *Newsweek* Telecommunications Forum less than two weeks after the signing of the TCA. He summarized the TCA quite simply by stating, "The goal of the Telecommunications Act is to let anyone enter any communications business—to let any communications business compete in any market against any other. The goal is to remove the legal and economic obstacles that have frustrated competition for too long." To make his point, Hundt quoted the title of his column on the Federal Trade Commission's WWW home page: "It's the end of the world as we know it."

Actually, the TCA goes beyond simply allowing competition. It sets the goals of the competition and gives the FCC the power to make the rules to achieve those goals. It also has two very controversial sections that address the transmission of obscene and violent material.

To understand the TCA better, we must examine its major points. The act has seven major thrusts that do not necessarily correspond to specific sections of the act because a specific thrust may transcend more than one section.

Interconnection

Under the TCA, all telecommunications carriers are obligated to interconnect with other telecommunications carriers. Also, they may not install network elements that interfere with such interconnections. To achieve the connection between the telecommunications network and individual homes, businesses, and so on, the local telephone companies have several specific additional obligations.

These include: (1) allowing the resale of its telecommunications services; (2) allowing number portability—a customer can keep the old phone number as he or she moves from one provider to another; (3) providing dialing parity—additional numbers need not be entered when affiliating with one telecommunications carrier as opposed to another; (4) offering access to right-of-ways, poles, ducts, and so forth at reasonable rates; and (5) providing reciprocal compensation arrangements. Besides these requirements, the TCA places requirements on existing (incumbent) local telephone companies. It also states the procedures for achieving these goals and the role the FCC and state commissions play in setting policies to accomplish the aims.

Removal of Barriers to Entry

In the specific words of the TCA, "No State or local statute or regulation or other State or local legal requirement, may prohibit or have the effect of prohibiting the ability of any entity to provide any interstate or intrastate telecommunications service" (47 USC 253). Restrictions apply regarding state regulation of the telecommunications industry. States can still impose requirements in the telecommunications industry; they must simply do so on a competitive, neutral basis and in a way that is consistent with the provisions of the TCA.

Universal Service

A significant portion of the TCA is to ensure *universal service*. This means that all areas of the country have equal access to comparable telecommunications services at "just, reasonable, and affordable rates." This section of the code is particularly designed to ensure that rural and low-income consumers have reasonably priced access to informational services. Under this part of the code, telecommunications companies may be required to provide service, at uninflated rates, to areas that might not be served if markets alone prevailed.

Under the TCA, telecommunications services and products must be manufactured for disabled individuals. Further, the TCA explicitly discusses health care and education. Health care workers, particularly those in rural areas, must have access to telecommunications services comparable to, and at rates comparable to, those in nonrural areas. In addition, primary and secondary schools must have access to telecommunications services at a reduced rate.

New Freedom for the Bell Operating Companies

As mentioned earlier, the Modified Final Judgment of 1984 broke up AT&T. AT&T subsequently specialized in manufacturing equipment and providing long-distance service, and the Bell operating companies provided local service. Except for specifically defined shorter long-distance calls (intralata calls), these RHCs were prohibited from providing long-distance service. For years, the

RHCs wanted to get into the longer-distance (interlata) market. The TCA gives them the opportunity to do so.

However, Congress wanted to be certain that, before these local exchange carriers began competing within their own regions for interlata long-distance customers, they had opened their local markets for competition. Therefore, the TCA stated that these RHCs must either have direct competition for local customers or have no requests to become competitors for ten months. The RHCs must then meet a fourteen-point checklist to ensure parity and interconnectivity with the competing companies. They could then start providing regional interlata long-distance services, although there is a period of time before they can sell this long-distance service along with their local telephone services.

Upon meeting these requirements, the RHCs may also begin developing and manufacturing telecommunications equipment. There are restrictions concerning other aspects of competition as well. For example, all Bell operating companies, except Ameritech, which previously won the right to provide burglar alarm monitoring services from the federal court overseeing the AT&T consent decree, are prohibited from entering the alarm monitoring business for five years after the enactment of the TCA.

Lessening of Broadcast Restrictions

There are various provisions in the TCA that affect ownership of the airways. For starters, there are provisions that open the airways for advanced television services. This will make high-definition broadcasts possible. It is not yet clear how receptive consumers will be to such services; thus, the FCC will review whether or not consumers are actually using them. The sole purpose of this section is to provide broadcast spectrum flexibility.

More important than these provisions are the sections that ease or eliminate broadcast ownership restrictions; the TCA opens up the radio and television broadcast industries for acquisitions, mergers, and expansions. There are only minor restrictions to the size of any given company; these limits are adequate to maintain competition and keep any given company from dominating a particular market.

Cable Reform

In 1992 Congress (over the veto of President Bush) passed the Cable Act, which repealed the 1984 deregulation of the cable television industry. This act subjected cable systems to rate regulations and a host of other FCC-enforced obligations. Criticisms lodged by disgruntled consumers and cable operators alike prompted the TCA. Price regulation will be phased out by the end of this decade.

Consistent with its theme of eliminating barriers to competition, the TCA opens up competition between cable companies and telephone companies. However, several provisions ensure that such competition does not result from telephone companies and cable companies buying out each other.

Violence and Obscenity

Overall the TCA was well received; however, controversy has arisen over its position on violence and obscenity. The last major section of the TCA deals with the transmission of violent and sexually explicit material. There are also a few miscellaneous provisions throughout the act that relate to sexually explicit and violent material. These sections have been the target of public criticism and legal maneuvering (Bradner 1996; Messmer 1996).

The sections primarily call for the reduction or elimination of children's access to violent and sexually explicit material. It is difficult to do this without, at minimum, inconveniencing all adults, and critics see almost any effort to do so as infringing upon their constitutional rights. And so a battle has ensued both in court and in the arena of public opinion. As of this writing, little has been resolved on either battlefield.

There are three primary ways that the law is attempting to accomplish its purpose. They vary in their degree of required government intervention. At one extreme is the approach that technology will take care of itself. The V-chip allows programs to be electronically screened, enabling parents to black out programs that might have inappropriate content for children. Under the TCA, television equipment manufacturers are required to equip all new TVs with the V-chip. When this is combined with a rating system for violent and sexually explicit material, parents will be able to categorically eliminate access to whole categories of television programs.

At the other extreme is the belief that prosecution will inhibit certain activities. The act imposes criminal penalties for the knowing transmission over the Internet of material considered indecent to minors. These provisions also make it a crime to transmit any material with the intent to annoy or harass the recipient.

In between, there is the approach that industries can regulate themselves. There is no mandate that broadcasters must develop the rating system needed for the implementation of the V-chip. However, the FCC is authorized to require rating transmission if the industry does not voluntarily begin to do so within one year. This may have had an effect: less than one month after the signing of the act, leaders from the entertainment industry met with President Clinton. They developed concrete guidelines for developing a rating system similar to that used in the motion picture industry. This system will be the foundation for self-regulation.

It is unlikely that the courts will veto all provisions of the anti-obscenity/ violence sections of the TCA. The Supreme Court has clearly said that obscene material does not have full First Amendment protection (Muncy 1992). The high court has not given people free reign to produce, distribute, or consume sexually explicit material in traditional ways. It is unlikely that they will suddenly open the airways and lines to the free flow of such material, particularly when it is difficult to monitor the more vulnerable members of our society. So, it is probably a safe assumption that most of the anti-obscenity/violence sections of the TCA will stay intact.

BRAND PARITY IN THE TELECOMMUNICATIONS INDUSTRY

What does all of this mean for marketing within the telecommunications industry in the future? Predictions abound as to what could happen. Mulqueen (1996) observes that prices for various telecommunications services will likely fall by 10 to 40 percent. Rohde and Messmer (1996) believe that competition will come two to three times quicker in the local markets than in the long-distance markets. Guy (1996) foresees many acquisitions and mergers in the industry. For example, there are as many as 600 to 700 long-distance companies in the United States. Many of these would be acquisition candidates.

Probably the most significant implication is that the telecommunications industry will become a high-parity industry. In the drive to increase competition, the government has in essence mandated product parity. Thus, it is extremely useful to understand brand parity to grasp how the TCA may impact on the industry.

Perceived brand parity has been defined as the overall belief held by consumers that the differences between the major brand alternatives in a product category are small (Muncy 1996). Thus, when consumers perceive the major brand alternatives as similar, parity is high. Conversely, when consumers perceive the alternatives as dissimilar, parity is low.

Parity can be seen as the opposite of product differentiation and, as noted by Kottman (1977), product differentiation is the "*sine qua non* of successful marketing" (p. 146). Kottman further stated that "the idea of parity is an anathema in marketing. It is antithetical to the notion of differentiation, and product differentiation is regarded as the lifeblood of successful national brand marketing and advertising" (p. 146). These opinions have been echoed by several leading marketing and advertising practitioners (see, for example, Giges 1988; Kanter 1981; Sloan 1989).

Is this concern justified? Based on intuition it seems so. Very often the primary goal of a marketing program is to create a customer base that is cognitively brand loyal and insensitive to price competition. However, such a customer base may be difficult to develop without perceived differences between major brand alternatives. Few consumers would likely say, "I am going to be loyal to a specific brand, although all of the major brands in the product category are alike." Neither does it seem likely that a customer would be willing to pay a higher price for a particular brand when the major alternatives in a product category are all the same.

In a similar way, customers seem insensitive to marketplace information about products of high brand parity. Muncy (1990) discusses a research study that found a strong relationship between perceived brand differences and information

Figure 4.1
A Model of the Effects of Brand Parity

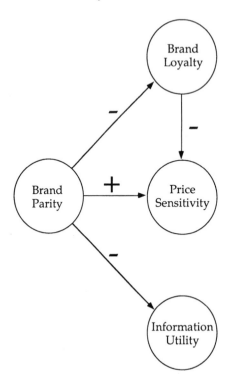

search. He explained these findings by stating that ''it is only when the consumer perceives that differences actually do exist that he or she is motivated to find out information about what these differences are'' (p. 146). Others have also argued that consumers are less receptive to advertising when high-parity perceptions exist (Giges 1988). If consumers are less receptive to marketing communications when parity perceptions are high, then they may not even give advertisers the opportunity to present information that could change such parity perceptions. Thus, battling brand parity may be confounded by its own existence.

Given all of the difficulties created by high-parity perceptions, it is not surprising that Allen Rosenshine, the President and CEO of the Omicon Group (BBDO's parent company), stated that it is the ''very purpose of advertising to differentiate brands in the consumer's mind and to reduce brand parity where it does exist'' (Giges 1988, p. 68). When a firm can successfully differentiate itself in the consumer's mind, then it is diminishing brand parity.

Muncy (1996) developed a model showing the effects of high levels of parity. A simplification of that model is presented in Figure 4.1. It states that high-parity consumers are much less likely to become brand loyal, they are much less sensitive to marketplace information, and they become much more price sensitive. All these spell trouble for the person trying to sell in a parity market. When consumers are not loyal, customer acquisition costs skyrocket, and the length of time one can expect to keep a customer diminishes. This is already happening in the long-distance segment of the telecommunications industry. Also, when consumers are not receptive to marketplace information (e.g., advertising), then traditional methods for communicating with them are gone. Innovative strategies must be developed.

The most troublesome aspect of brand parity is probably in the relationship between brand parity and price sensitivity. As consumers increase their degree of perceived parity, they become much more price sensitive. They are willing to switch products to get a lower price. In fact, they start demanding lower prices. This makes an industry do one of two things. They must either think of ways to decrease these parity perceptions or resign themselves to price competition. When competition is based solely on price and when no company has a particular cost advantage, then industry profits are not likely to be strong.

IMPLICATIONS FOR MARKETING IN THE TELECOMMUNICATIONS INDUSTRY

Are low profits the unavoidable fate of the telecommunications industry? That may be a pessimistic prognosis for an industry in a state of elation over its newfound competitive freedom. The answer is clearly no. Some companies are likely to do well, even thrive, in this industry. However, others are likely to experience a disappointing, if not devastating, future. What will be the difference? The ability to successfully market products in ways that will differentiate them from the competition. Two measures are needed. First, firms must break free from their existing paradigms. Second, they must find new ones that are uniquely suited to their company strengths.

Thomas Kuhn (1962) popularized the word *paradigm*. He maintained that scientists reach a point where they can no longer progress because they are so vested in the existing variables, structures, methodologies, and theories of their existing world that they cannot see different ones that develop. Until someone comes along who looks at the world in a totally different way, scientists are bound by their existing paradigms. For example, Einstein did not simply add onto Newtonian physics: He redefined the paradigm. His theory of relativity allowed physicists to break free from their existing paradigm and see the world differently. Then and only then could the field of physics progress.

I see two paradigms that will be particularly difficult to renounce. The first is the regulatory paradigm. Everything from geographic expansions to pricing has been under steep regulatory influence. The legal department is much more important than the marketing department, in terms of a company's revenue, in such an environment. But that is all about to change because consumers, not regulatory agencies, will determine price. The ability to compete, not the ability to negotiate, will determine geographic expansion.

The world of politics is difficult but at least somewhat civil. The world of competition is absolutely ruthless. There is no arbitrating body. If consumers vote yes with their dollars, then companies are allowed to continue. If they vote no, companies have no choice but to shut down. No amount of pleading, negotiating, contributing, wining and dining, or legal maneuvering will save a company's bottom line, unless it can collect and maintain customers. Firms that have been in the somewhat predictable arena of government regulation are in for a surprise as the fast-paced world of competition invades their markets. The world as they knew it is gone forever.

The other paradigm that must be avoided is the paradigm of the past. Firms that have been under heavy government regulation and are suddenly thrust into a competitive world will be tempted to adopt the paradigms of other industries. Heavy advertising, direct mail, and telemarketing will all be tried extensively to attract mass numbers of customers. However, they may be absolutely useless because of the brand parity dictated by the TCA. Hence, the structure of the industry has moved from almost pure monopoly to almost pure competition. Accepting without question the tools used in markets of monopolistic competition is not the solution. Innovative approaches are needed.

Two strategies that have worked particularly well in the long-distance segment of the telecommunications industry are worth discussing. One is niche marketing and the other is network marketing. Niche marketing occurs when a firm goes after a relatively small but well-defined group of customers. Let us look at how this was done in the long-distance market.

In 1984, AT&T began targeting the gay market by supporting the gay games. It followed with a direct-mail campaign that touted its gay employees. MCI soon reacted. It helped launch the National Gay and Lesbian Business Alliance and sent a mailing to gay business owners, offering them a six-month membership in the alliance worth $39 if they signed up with MCI.

While AT&T was targeting gays, an Oklahoma City upstart long-distance company called Lifeline developed a strong customer base by targeting conservative Christians. It made a donation to charitable causes, such as churches, Christian schools, Christian radio stations, and pro-life organizations, based on customers long-distance usage. Customers were willing to sign up and stay with Lifeline, although other companies offered much lower rates. The customers' loyalty to their religion was projected onto their loyalty to their long-distance company.

These are but two examples of pursuing well-defined niches in long-distance markets. Note that the service is the same. What differs is attaching some benefit beyond the product's scope to attract consumers.

Another approach that is extremely successful in developing customer loyalty is network marketing, also called multilevel marketing. This technique is quickly becoming the marketing technique of choice for many leaders in certain industries (Poe 1995). Two of the fastest-growing companies in the industry, Excel Telecommunications and LCI, are succeeding specifically through network marketing.

With network marketing, people receive compensation for recruiting customers and for recruiting others to do the same. For example, Excel Telecommunications requires their Independent Representatives to gather twenty customer points (any given customer may count for anywhere from one to four customer points). Representatives also become eligible for bonuses as they recruit other customers. These bonuses can range from $25 to $265. This can add up to large sums of money for those who can supply a few customers and encourage others to do the same.

Network marketing is attractive within the long-distance industry because loyalty is tied to an individual, not to a company. A person recruits his or her parents as customers not because of the service or the price but because he or she receives additional compensation. Customers remain loyal because they are loyal to the representative; this is how firms maintain a loyal customer base in a high-parity industry.

CONCLUSION

Niche marketing and network marketing are not the only techniques that will be effective in the new world created by the TCA. They are but two examples typically ignored by large consumer-goods companies when selling to large segments of the market. They have proven extremely effective in selling long-distance service and there is no reason that they should be unsuited to selling to other segments of the industry. But companies will undoubtedly develop other techniques, such as product bundling. Several products, such as cable, long distance, home security, paging, and cellular phones, may be sold together for a low price.

The point to remember is that Congress has never mandated into existence a parity industry the size of what has occurred through the TCA. Many large firms must now break away from their existing paradigms of government regulation and compete through marketing in an arena that is inherently difficult. This should tax the creative and analytical marketing skills of all involved to the maximum degree possible. The prize is large for those who succeed. Obscurity is the fate for all who fail.

5

The High-Tech Innovator: A Model and Scale for Measurement

Jacqueline K. Eastman

This chapter will help high-technology organizations better understand how innovativeness works and how to measure and predict who is an innovator. I will describe a model of innovativeness (Goldsmith et al. 1995); present a domain-specific measure of innovativeness (Goldsmith and Hofacker (1991); illustrate the use of this measure in several studies (Goldsmith and Flynn 1992; Flynn and Goldsmith 1993a; Flynn and Goldsmith 1993b; Goldsmith and Flynn 1993–1994; and Goldsmith et al. 1996); and apply the idea and measure of innovativeness specifically to the high-tech consumer (Ellen et al. 1991).

Innovation is very expensive for high-technology firms because they must spend their money and time on developing the next generation of products (Weinig 1990). "Firms are continually reminded that technological innovations within the firm and for its customers are key to their success and survival in a highly competitive environment" (Ellen et al. 1991, p. 297; Taylor 1987). Hayward (1981, p. 158) suggests three essentials needed for innovation: (1) the presence and actions of the innovator; (2) better understanding between the innovator and private-venture capital sources; and (3) greater emphasis on curricula related to innovation and entrepreneurship. High technology is not only a product, but also a process to more accurately target consumers. Direct marketing firms need to be early innovators (Roscitt and Parker 1988). Elliot (1989) offers that innovation is a rational process and that the evolution of technology can be a predictable process. Although the benefits of technology may be evident to the firm, the end users may be less receptive to technological innovation (Ellen et al. 1991; Blackler and Brown 1985). Firms need to recognize that high-tech businesses "typically have high research and development costs, high market growth, short product life cycles, and offer the opportunity to change the fundamental structure of the existing business" ("Managing High-Tech

Portfolio'' 1979, p. 6). Given the resources needed for a firm to be innovative, it is critical to understand this process.

"Because of the typically short life cycle of high-technology products, which results in limited time to sell in depth to the potential adopter population, the identification of prospective buyers is important'' (Johne 1984, p. 59). Midgley (1977) stresses that the key to successful new product introduction is marketing the product to the minority of consumers who are the first to buy in a given product market (Goldsmith and Flynn 1992). Johne (1984, p. 59) suggests that product innovation practices can be used effectively as a basis to segment markets. "Unfortunately, marketers have not had a simple, reliable method for identifying consumer innovators before a product launch'' (Goldsmith and Flynn 1992, p. 42). With the large outlay of resources, the firm needs to have a stronger idea of who comprises their customer base.

A MODEL OF INNOVATIVENESS

According to Kassarjian (1971) and others (Kassarjian and Sheffet 1981; Foxall and Goldsmith 1988), personality research has suffered from several conceptual and methodological weaknesses. In looking at the personality trait of innovativeness specifically, there has been a problem with "the level of generality/specificity or abstraction at which the relevant constructs are conceptualized and measured,'' and when this oversight is corrected, the personality construct of innovativeness can be modeled more effectively (Goldsmith et al. 1995, pp. 601–602). Goldsmith et al. (1995) hypothesized that a more abstract trait of innovativeness (such as global innovativeness) would have a weaker correlation with innovative behavior in a particular area than a domain-specific measure of innovativeness.

"Personality psychologists recognize that global, abstract constructs may be more useful in predicting lower-level abstract constructs than in predicting overt behavior. The more abstract the trait, the lower its predictive validity'' (Goldsmith et al. 1995, p. 603). Narrowly defined traits, however, tend to be better predictors of particular behavior (Buss 1989). Thus, several theories exist that describe the relationships among abstract concepts to specific behaviors, with domain-specific constructs in the middle acting as mediator variables (Brown 1989; Goldsmith et al. 1995).

Midgley and Dowling (1978) address the importance of recognizing the abstraction at which innovativeness is conceptualized and measured. They suggest three levels of innovativeness: (1) innate innovativeness, "the degree to which an individual makes innovation decisions independently of the communicated experiences of others'' (p. 235); (2) specific innovativeness for a product category (domain-specific); and (3) specific innovativeness for a single product that interacts with situational variables. Midgley and Dowling (1978) recognize that there is a hierarchical flow of influence from the most abstract construct, innate

Figure 5.1
Model of Innovativeness

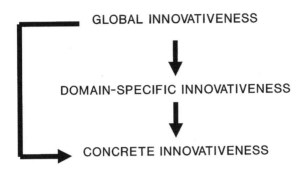

innovativeness, to the most concrete, actual product adoption, just as personality psychologists suggest (Goldsmith et al. 1995, p. 605). It is critical that both domain-specific and global (innate) innovativeness are measured at the proper level of abstraction for best results (Goldsmith et al. 1995). Yet, while Midgley and Dowling (1978) support the hierarchical model of innovativeness, from abstract to domain-specific, they fail to adequately specify the operationalization needed to test this model (Goldsmith et al. 1995, p. 605).

Hirschman (1980) also claims that innate innovativeness may account for individual differences in adoption behavior but calls this construct "inherent novelty seeking," arguing that "the desire to seek out the new and different (i.e., inherent novelty seeking) is conceptually indistinguishable from the willingness to adopt new products (i.e., inherent innovativeness)" (p. 285). Hirschman, however, fails to address the intermediate conceptual level of domain-specific innovativeness; instead she offers that inherent novelty seeking and creativity work with other variables to account for differences in product adoption behavior (Goldsmith and Flynn 1992). Thus, Hirschman's theory does not adequately address how innovative behaviors could be predicted, that is, how high-tech consumers will act.

Goldsmith et al. (1995) propose a model for innovativeness (see Figure 5.1). First, global innovativeness is conceptualized as an abstract personality trait, equivalent to Midgley and Dowling's (1978) "innate innovativeness"; it is correlated positively with the less abstract concept of domain-specific innovativeness, and to a lesser extent to a pattern of concrete adoption behaviors (Midgley and Dowling's actualized innovativeness) because it is further away in terms of level of abstraction (Goldsmith et al. 1995, p. 605). "Second, the domain-specific measure is correlated more highly with the concrete behavior than the global concept (again, because it is closer in level of abstraction). Third, the relationship between the global trait and the concrete behavior is mediated by the domain-specific measure" (Goldsmith et al. 1995, p. 606).

Goldsmith et al. (1995) test this theory through surveying 462 subjects (225

Table 5.1
Measures of Global Innovativeness

GLOBAL INNOVATIVENESS (Hurt, Joseph, and Cook 1977)

1.   I am reluctant about adopting new ways of doing things until
      I see them working for people around me.
2.   I rarely trust new ideas until I can see whether the vast
      majority of people around me accept them.
3.   I am aware that I am usually one of the last people in my
      group to accept something new.
4.   I must see other people using new innovations before I will
      consider them.
5.   I am generally cautious about accepting new ideas.
6.   I tend to feel that the old way of living and doing things
      is the best way.

DOMAIN-SPECIFIC INNOVATIVENESS (Goldsmith and Hofacker 1991)
(insert domain, such as new electronic entertainment equipment or
new fashion items)

1.   In general, I am the last (first) in my circle of friends to
      know about the latest _____.
2.   Compared to my friends, I own few of (a lot of) _____.
3.   In general, I am among the first (last) in my circle of
      friends to buy a _____ when it appears.
4.   I (do not) like to buy a _____ before other
      people do.
5.   If I heard that a _____ was available in
      the store, I would (not) be interested enough to buy it.
6.   I will not buy a _____ if I haven't
      heard/tried it yet.(I will buy a new _____ if I
      haven't heard/tried it yet).

Note: Words/sentences in parentheses denote the positive and negative wording for the individual
   items as both positive or negative versions of each item has been developed.

men and 237 women) between the ages of 24 and 60 in a southeastern U.S.
mall catering to upper-middle-class households. The interviews focused on attitudes and behaviors regarding personal fashion and household electronic equipment because these two categories are diverse enough to examine both
generalized innovativeness and domain-specific innovativeness. The data gathered included demographic data; global innovativeness (see Table 5.1), as measured by Hurt et al. (1977), that taps into a consumer "willingness to try new
things" (Goldsmith 1991, p. 89); domain-specific innovativeness (see Table
5.1), as measured by Goldsmith and Hofacker (1991) for both fashionable cloth-
ing and electronic entertainment equipment; and concrete or actualized innovativeness, which was measured by presenting the respondents with a list of six
fashion and six electronic innovations and asking the respondents if they owned
these products.

The study by Goldsmith et al. (1995, p. 609) found, as hypothesized by the
model and as shown in Figure 5.1, that "there were weak positive correlations

between global innovativeness and purchase of new products . . . also, as hypothesized, there were stronger correlations between the domain-specific innovativeness measures and their purchase measures. Finally, the correlations between global innovativeness and purchases were reduced almost to zero when the mediating effects of domain-specific innovativeness were removed." Goldsmith et al. prove that their model is a strong means of predicting innovative behavior. This knowledge can aid marketing managers in capturing the innovative, high-tech consumer because managers will find a stronger rate of success in introducing new products by targeting domain-specific innovators for their product category, rather than by targeting a global innovator. In the next section, I describe in more detail the development of the domain-specific measure of innovativeness.

A DOMAIN-SPECIFIC MEASURE OF INNOVATIVENESS

Consumer innovativeness has been typically assessed using one of three strategies: time-of-adoption measures (Rogers 1962), the cross-sectional method, or some form of self-report (Kohn and Jacoby 1973). Regarding time-of-adoption measures, Rogers and Shoemaker (1971, p. 27) define innovativeness as the "degree to which an individual is relatively earlier in adopting an innovation than other members of his system." Researchers have used time-of-adoption "to assign consumers to the adopter categories based on some arbitrary categorization scheme" (Goldsmith and Hofacker 1991, p. 209). The use of time-of-adoption has been criticized because reliability, validity, and generalizability cannot be determined (Hurt et al. 1977; Midgley and Dowling 1978).

Instead of time-of-adoption, Midgley and Dowling (1978, p. 230) propose that the cross-sectional method, "determining how many of a pre-specified list of new products a particular individual has purchased at the time of the survey," is a better measure of innate innovativeness. This method, however, only measures actual innovative behaviors and does not tap into the personality trait of innovativeness. Further, it does not address the study of innovativeness in a specific domain nor that innovativeness does not seem to overlap across domains (Gatignon and Robertson 1985). "In summary, it would be desirable to have a simple, easily administered scale to measure consumer innovativeness that could be adapted to any domain of interest and used in surveys" (Goldsmith and Hofacker 1991, p. 210).

Goldsmith and Hofacker (1991) describe the six studies they used to develop and validate their domain-specific innovativeness scale (the DSI—see Table 5.1). The scale development followed Churchill's (1979) paradigm. In Study One, an initial survey of eleven items was created based on a literature review (rock music products were the domain used); the final six items of the DSI were derived through item analysis, coefficient alpha, and criterion validity (Bearden et al. 1993). Study Two further looked at the reliability, validity, and unidimensional factor structure of the DSI (again with rock music). Studies Three and Four further examined the scale's psychometric properties using the domains of fashion and household entertainment equipment. Study Five looked at the test-retest reliability, predictive validity, and possible confounds of the scale (again with rock music as the domain). Finally, Study Six addressed the convergent and discriminant validity of the scale using the domains of cologne, perfume, and aftershave. Students were used in Studies One, Two, Three, Five, and Six; nonstudents were used in Studies Four and Six (Goldsmith and Hofacker 1991; Bearden et al. 1993, p. 59). The results of the studies illustrated that the DSI was unidimensional and reliable, with strong criterion and predictive validity as well as convergent and discriminant validity.

Since the development of the DSI scale, Goldsmith and others have shown the usefulness of this scale in measuring domain-specific innovativeness and predicting domain-specific innovative behaviors. This discussion will help set the foundation for how this scale can be used to attract the high-tech consumer.

With the DSI scale, Goldsmith and Flynn (1992) showed that women can be classified as innovators or non-innovators of fashion. Those who were in the innovator group were found to both shop more and spend more on fashion. This has tremendous implications for fashion retailers; it stresses the need to update inventory and displays to lure the innovative fashion consumer. Additionally, fashion innovators were more likely to read fashion magazines, fashion stories in the newspaper, and watch television shows dealing with new fashions. Thus, this market segment could be easily reached with a variety of media sources. The advertisements need to focus on the innovative buyer because they buy first, more often, and spend a higher dollar amount. Finally, these consumers were also more interested in style than practicality and needed assistance from knowledgeable salespeople. The DSI is able to discern fashion innovators and, determine what they need from fashion marketers. This type of study could also be done with high-tech consumer-product domains.

Flynn and Goldsmith (1993a) showed the usefulness of the DSI in determining the innovator of consumer travel services. Those adults who scored higher on the DSI for travel services took more vacation trips and made greater use of travel agents. As with the fashion study, the need for new displays, new inventory, and highly trained sales and service people was evident. Likewise with the fashion study (Goldsmith and Flynn 1992), the innovators of travel services were more likely to read magazines, newspaper articles, and watch television programs that dealt with travel than non-innovative travelers. Thus, the innovative consumer for a particular domain can be reached through mass media sources. Additionally, the travel innovator, like the fashion innovator, was interested in attending shows dealing with their domain of interest to learn what was new in that area. Furthermore, it is important to note that travel innovators "were not distinguishable from the later adopter in terms of age, education, household income, or even vacation home ownership and travel club membership" (Flynn and Goldsmith 1993a, p. 108). Finally, Goldsmith and Flynn (1993–1994) note that innovative vacationers are likely to be more involved with, more knowledgeable about, and more opinionated about vacation travel than non-innovative vacationers.

Through looking at rock music and undergraduates, Flynn and Goldsmith (1993b) found that "rock music innovativeness was positively associated with opinion leadership for, involvement with, and both perceived and real knowledge of rock music. Innovativeness was also positively associated with a rock music magazine readership, time spent shopping for rock records, money spent for rock records, and time spent listening to the rock music" (p. 1105). Thus, rock music innovators show a similar pattern of behavior as previously found for adults in the domains of fashion and travel. Innovators can aid marketers by endorsing products through word of mouth. Thus, they are a critical segment of the market to reach, and with the DSI they can be assessed in a simple six-item reliable and valid measure. Additionally, Flynn and Goldsmith (1993b) suggest that the DSI measure could easily be adopted to other domains and even nonconsumer areas, where innovations appear with some frequency. Thus, high-tech products for both consumers and industrial markets would be applicable to the DSI.

Finally, Goldsmith et al. (1996) report that undergraduate innovators of fashion tended to be highly involved, opinionated leaders of fashion; they have a higher level of perceived knowledge regarding fashion; exhibit more shopping and spending habits regarding fashion; and are more motivated to consume for status purposes than non-innovators.

As the studies described above illustrate, the construct of domain-specific innovativeness is related to several other personality constructs and behaviors in a way that cannot be explained by demographic variables.

REACHING THE HIGH-TECH CONSUMER

Marketing researchers have called for increased attention on consumer resistance to new products, particularly those that are high-tech (Gatignon and Robertson 1989; Ellen et al. 1991). Ellen et al. (1991, p. 305) report two sources of resistance to technological innovations: (1) self-efficacy (i.e., consumers' perceived ability to change), with those who felt high self-efficacy being less resistant to change; and (2) performance satisfaction, with those who were less satisfied with current product performance being less resistant to change. Thus, given the resources involved in new product development, particularly those in the high-tech arena, and the risk for failure, it is critical that firms tap into the innovator for their product category.

CONCLUSION

This chapter points out the need to model innovativeness on a general construct (global innovativeness) that leads to domain-specific innovativeness and finally yields actual innovative behavior in a particular domain. Additionally, this chapter highlights Goldsmith and Hofacker's (1991) DSI scale, a unidimensional, reliable, and valid measure that can be adopted to different product domains. This chapter further illustrates the success of this scale in predicting innovative behaviors better than demographic measures and shows that the scale is related to many other personality constructs that help identify and reach innovative consumers. This chapter explains that innovators also tend to be opinion leaders (endorsing by word of mouth a product's value) who are involved in the domain; have a high level of perceived knowledge; and who are motivated to consume for status.

To conclude, Goldsmith and Hofacker's (1991) scale can be used by high-tech firms to determine their innovative consumers and how they can best target these potential buyers.

6

Quality and the High-Tech Consumer

Claude R. Superville and Allan C. Reddy

This chapter presents aspects of quality and quality control in the realm of high-tech markets and high-tech marketing. Having quality products and services has become extremely important for success in business today. Without quality in products and services, marketers are ineffective in selling them.

There are arguable aspects to the revolution known as Total Quality Management (TQM) that are directly applicable to the high-technology consumer. This management approach emphasizes Japanese quality-management techniques and the contributions of American quality gurus such as W. Edwards Deming, Joseph Juran, and others. Statistical Quality Control (SQC), the second approach, emphasizes the role of statistical tools and techniques in improving the quality of goods and services received by consumers. Both aspects of TQM are examined here.

QUALITY MANAGEMENT

The major thrust for the quality movement came from Japan. Several recent innovations, such as Quality Control (Q) Circles, developed in the late 1950s and early 1960s, were invented by the Japanese. They successfully carried out these ideas because they had strong support from various government organizations, such as the Union of Japanese Scientists and Engineers, the Ministry for International Trade and Industry (MITI), and the powerful business associations. One important Japanese innovation in their relentless pursuit of quality was the Q circle.

Quality Control (Q) Circles

Q circles are small groups of employees doing similar work under one supervisor; they meet regularly to identify, analyze, and solve quality problems

(Rieker 1977). They are participatory problem-solving groups. The circles follow the theory that people will take more interest in and value their work if they are allowed to decide their work. Furthermore, this theory assumes that those who work on a particular job know the best way to make improvements (Harnac and Brannen 1982, pp. 67–68).

Theoretically, Q circles are voluntary. Each circle consists of about ten people and meets weekly. Training both leaders and members involves learning various techniques used when giving a management presentation. In addition, the training includes brainstorming, cause-and-effect diagrams, Pareto diagrams, histograms, check sheets, graphs, sampling, and control charts to analyze the sources and cause of quality problems.

Introduced into the United States in the mid-1980s, Q circles have not been as effective as they are in Japan because of social and cultural differences (Callahan 1982, p. 107). In the United States, workers are individualistic and self-centered, whereas in Japan, they are group-centered and self-sacrificing. Thus, Q circles work better in Japan and similar social environments.

A concept such as quality circles is easy to understand. To operationalize these ideas, however, each country must develop its own system that corresponds to its distinct social and cultural environment. Certain subjective factors, such as unique social and cultural characteristics, can often influence a country's economic competitiveness and achievement. For example, in Japan, the interaction of three major behavioral variables—attitudes toward work, achievement, and adaptability—enabled them to achieve the 'economic miracle' (Reddy et al. 1984, p. 45). The Japanese model is now being emulated by other East Asian countries, which share similar social and cultural characteristics, with impressive success.

Poka-Yoke

Japanese quality expert Shiego Shingo introduced an idea called poka-yoke, a way to reduce human error. For instance, if a car's headlights were so designed to make them look awkward when installed, poka-yoke would call for change in the design. United Electric Controls Company, a maker of industrial sensors and controls in Watertown, Massachusetts, and a recent Shingo convert, has added beveled edges to parts so that they can only be assembled the correct way, helping slash delivery time from twelve weeks to three days. These ideas relate to production quality directly, but are also applicable to marketing quality in terms of the approach and discipline needed to maintain consistent quality.

A more radical approach comes from Genichi Taguchi, a well-known Japanese engineering consultant. He calls it "robust design." Taguchi argues (Taguchi and Clausing 1990) that missing the quality target consistently is better than hitting it, at least when allowable deviations are scattered throughout the area. He uses the analogy of two sharpshooters: one always hits a 6-inch-diameter bull's-eye, but the shots are scattered from edge to edge. The other hits the bull's-eye less often, but all the shots are grouped in a 3-inch circle. The latter would win without competition if he adjusts his rifle's sights.

Consistency is critical. Taguchi insists, because of a rule of thumb called the quality loss function, that any deviation from the dead center, no matter how small, increases a product's ultimate costs, including warranty liability and lost customer goodwill. Taguchi's insights have been a staple of Japanese engineering education for three decades. But they were almost unknown in the United States until 1983, when the Ford Motor Company began teaching them to its engineers. Only now are they widely embraced. This is why many U.S. and European manufacturers find themselves sitting where the Japanese were a decade or two ago ("The Quality Imperative" 1991, pp. 58–61).

According to Juran (1993), the Japanese did not learn about quality from him or Deming, contrary to what is generally believed to be true in the West. Juran believes that the idea of quality was inherent in the Japanese culture; he and Deming merely reinforced it. The Japanese had two types of quality: one for war machines and one for consumer goods. In World War II, their Zero aircraft and ammunition were of very high quality, but their consumer products were shoddy. After the war, they invested heavily in modernizing their factories and improving the quality of consumer goods to near perfection.

William Shanklin (1989, p. 28) asserts that improving product quality alone does not guarantee success and prosperity. Shanklin further believes that Frank Perdue built his family's small chicken-producing operation into the fifth largest company in its industry by observing quality in total marketing effort. Growth is achieved by combining a zeal for product quality with aggressive and innovative marketing, and by making right decisions and implementing them correctly every time.

Maytag is another company that has clearly proved quality sells in the marketplace. These days, however, consumers expect not only high quality in a given product or service, but also low price and other quality-driven marketing strategies. In today's global competition, replete with intense media scrutiny, no company can compete by selling shoddy products. Today's more educated and demanding consumers want to know "Where's the beef?", as asked in the classic Wendy's hamburgers advertisement.

Firms cannot survive selling the sizzle without the steak. Strong psychological appeals to people's needs and wants must be accompanied by intrinsic product quality for marketing to be effective. Steak without some sizzle does not usually attract customers, even in business-to-business marketing. But a sizzle without steak is a sure recipe for failure.

Emphasizing the glitter at the expense of quality has driven several American firms into deep trouble, especially with foreign competition. While Japanese automakers sold their cars on quality, value, and economy, during the 1970s and 1980s, U.S. automakers were using exotic promotions by appealing through movie celebrities, such as Farah Fawcett, to sell their cars.

All segments of consumers are alike in one important way, despite their varying lifestyles. Consumers want one thing—products that work and services that meet their needs.

A company can build a whole corporate strategy around quality. The issue of quality can be a common goal and a bond among all corporate functions—from production to sales and everything that supports them. Consequently, quality needs to be the daily concern of all employees, from the CEO to the newest hire in maintenance. This achievement is easier said than done, of course, and requires careful employee selection, constant employee training, and a facilitating corporate culture. Union-management relations at one prominent airline company became so strained that some employees decided to retaliate against management by doing their jobs poorly. No amount of training could rectify this kind of distrust (Shanklin 1989, pp. 37–38).

One should never advertise product quality if it is not there. Puffery and exaggeration are sure to come back to haunt the company that claims its products and services cannot be outdone. From a marketing standpoint, there is nothing worse than unconfirmed customer expectations (Shanklin 1989, p. 38). The Japanese companies assembling automobiles in the United States, such as Honda, Nissan, and others, outperform Ford in quality surveys of car owners. Ford says it has "designed" the best-quality cars and trucks in the United States; this is technically true: The Japanese cars are built in the United States but designed in Japan (Shanklin 1989, p. 39).

TQM is the only source of enduring competitive advantages in today's world. Pankaj Ghemwat (1986) categorizes these advantages into three groups: (1) size in the targeted market, (2) better access to resources and customers, and (3) restrictions on competitor options.

To exploit commitment opportunities, a business can preempt its competitors. The business, however, has to be especially wary of environmental changes that can erode the value of its early investments. Size can be beneficial only when there are compelling advantages to being large, such as economies of scale, scope, or experience. Advantages through preferred access to resources, information, or customers can give a business a sustainable advantage that is independent of size. Furthermore, restriction on options available to competitors might occasionally arise, limiting their ability to imitate the lead company's strategy. Rivals can be frozen into their current position by restrictive public policies, by their inability to defend their positions, and the response lags.

A survey in 1981 found that nearly 50 percent of American consumers felt that the quality of U.S. products dropped during the previous five years (Binstock 1981, p. 13). Another survey, Gallup in 1985, found that consumers would pay about one-third more for a better-quality car; 50 percent more for a better-quality dishwasher; proportionately more for a television or sofa; and twice the list price for better-quality shoes. The study also found that people with higher incomes were far more dissatisfied with the quality of American products (Peters 1987, p. 83).

"Quality" is thus fast becoming a primary competitive issue in the 1990s

(Garvin 1988). The label "Made in U.S.A." once represented an assurance of quality and reliability. Unfortunately, for many people in recent years, it has become a warning! As incidents of shoddy construction and defective products increase, dissatisfied consumers and industrial buyers turn to imports as alternatives. It is a pattern that cuts across all income and educational levels, ideologies, and national pride. Wealthy Americans want the German Mercedes and the budget-conscious prefer a Korean Hyundai. People who are most avid proponents of "Buy America" will buy Japanese appliances, Italian shoes, and Taiwanese sports clothes without hesitation.

The drive for higher quality is a result of several new factors. Modern consumers are better educated, more discriminating, more demanding, and are no longer intimidated by the store or the supplier. In addition, advances in technology make product quality and reliability normal, expected conditions (Kami 1988, p. 105).

Such quality problems are pervasive in most American firms, and are not limited to a single industry. Tom Peters, in his book *Thriving on Chaos*, points out, "For the most part, the quality of made-in-America goods and services is questionable; perhaps 'stinks' is often a more accurate word. Yet, fifteen years after the battering began, quality is still not often truly at the top of the American corporate agenda" (1987, p. 81).

Some experts warn that unless American firms match or better quality levels achieved by foreign competitors, the U.S. industry and the economy are bound to suffer. Yet, many American firms disregard this important message and ignore quality. According to a survey of several hundred large institutional investors, earnings ranked first and quality last among factors that influence stock selection (Factor 1985, p. 18).

From the viewpoint of customers, getting a defective product is a nuisance. Customers simply refuse to suffer the inconvenience of waiting for someone to fix the problem; instead, they will buy alternative brands with better quality and reputation. The Japanese experience clearly shows that manufacturing the product correctly in the first place is less costly than fixing it after customers buy it. Quality does not mean meeting assembly-line inspections standards during the manufacturing. Products have to be designed to meet customer needs from the start. One defective automobile part in 10,000 may not seem like much, but if that part keeps a completed car from starting at the end of the production line, finding the problem can be very costly.

Firms that adopted TQM methods to reduce manufacturing defects soon used the same approaches to overcome many other application problems. Their success brought attention to what is possible with TQM—whether the implementation problem concerns unreliable delivery schedules, poor customer service, advertising that appears on the wrong TV show, or salespeople who can't answer customers' questions. The idea of doing things right the first time seems obvious, but it's easier said than done.

THE QUALITY EXPERTS

Crosby

Philip Crosby defines quality as "conformance to requirements." In service companies, for example, "the waste goes out in baskets, and in manufacturing it goes out in barrels" (1979, p. 15).

Deming

W. Edwards Deming is a consultant and Distinguished Professor of Management at Columbia University. Born on October 14, 1900, in Sioux City, Iowa, he received his Ph.D. in mathematical physics at Yale University in 1928. He also received the Order of Sacred Treasure, Second Class (Japan) in 1960.

During the 1950s, Deming made several trips to Japan to instruct the Japanese on controlling quality in production. His important message was quality problems can be controlled through a rigorous and systematic statistical process. Going beyond statistical instruction, he encouraged firms to use a systematic approach to problem solving. This is known as "Plan, Do, Check, Action" (PDCA), or "Deming Cycle" (1982, pp. 101–104). He pushed top managers to get involved in the firm's quality programs and introduced modern methods of consumer research.

Juran

Joseph M. Juran is Chairperson Emeritus at Juran Institute, Inc. He was born on December 24, 1904, in Braila, Romania; he holds a B.S. degree in electrical engineering from the University of Minnesota and a J.D. degree from Loyola University. He too is a recipient of the Order of Sacred Treasure, Second Class.

Like Deming, Juran lectured in Japan during the 1950s. His lectures focused on planning, organizational issues, management's responsibility for quality, and the need to set goals and targets for general quality improvement on a project-by-project basis. Thus, Juran imbued in the minds of the Japanese the basic philosophy of planning quality (1974).

According to Juran (1993, pp. 35–38), we have a quality crisis. The guru of the international quality movement explains what is wrong with so many American efforts to employ TQM. Only a few of America's major companies have attained world-class quality—less than 50 of the Fortune 500; even fewer corporations in the general population have attained this goal. The remaining companies are in various stages of their quality journey. Some have not yet started. Some are starting over. Some have begun to make progress. Some are well along. Others have tried, failed, and given up.

The most dramatic evidence of the quality crisis in the Western world has been the superior quality of many Japanese products. Because of their quality revolution, Japanese manufacturers outperformed their Western competitors. Japan offered a higher quality of goods to the same customers for whom Western companies were competing, at equal or lower prices. That revolution did much damage to U.S. companies. It reduced their market shares, contributed to a severe decline in the balance of trade, and resulted in the export of many U.S. jobs.

There are other contributors to the quality crisis. One is the general growth of international competition, fueled by the rise of multinational companies. A more subtle contributor has been the growth of industrialized societies. Such societies redesign their lifestyles to secure the benefits of technological products. In turn, these societies require failure-free performance to maintain continuity of services, to protect against disruption in their lives, and to avoid disaster.

Why have the companies that tried to enact quality programs failed? Many CEOs of the 1980s realized that the quality crisis called for a solid response—a counterrevolution in quality. However, most of those CEOs did not know how to do this. They readily explain their ignorance.

About a century ago, the Taylor system of management, which separates planning from execution, emerged in the United States. Although it helped America become the world leader in productivity, the Taylor system was damaging to quality as it is known today. In response, U.S. companies created the central inspection department, which evolved into the quality departments of today. It became convenient to delegate the responsibility for quality to those departments. As a by-product, the CEOs became detached from, and ignorant of, the problems of managing for quality.

As the quality crisis grew, it took a growing toll on market shares. Because it would be wasteful to get into the free-trade-versus protectionism argument, companies must try to block imports and improve quality. The record shows that preoccupation with protectionism seldom improves competitiveness; sometimes it even damages public relations. During President Bush's 1992 visit to Japan, some CEOs of leading U.S. companies who went along with him in the trip complained that the Japanese market was closed to them. Naturally, the media focused on the spectacle of the American CEOs complaining at a time when they lacked right-side-drive cars to sell in Japan.

Unsuccessful companies did not consider that quality and customer satisfaction were fundamental. Unsuccessful companies did not include such quality-related goals as improving customer satisfaction, meeting competitive quality, reducing cost of poor quality, and improving major processes.

Unsuccessful companies did not use benchmarks for setting ambitious quality goals. In addition, many goals were ludicrously unattainable. These companies focused exclusively on financial measures—sales, profits, return on investment—and lacked two essential measures of quality: measures of customer satisfaction and competitive quality. Lacking these, they learned of their quality problems only after severe damage had occurred. Also, these firms did not establish a regular executive review of performance against the quality goals that paralleled the review of performance against the financial goals.

Indeed, unsuccessful companies did not conduct self-audits. They did not identify the strengths and weaknesses of the divisions and the support services. Thus, none of this information was available to guide their decisions. Companies that did attempt such self-audits failed to measure against strict and uniform criteria.

Many companies did not give public acknowledgement to persons and teams that achieved superior performance. Also, they did not revise the reward system to reflect the job changes inherent in the quality initiative. Furthermore, they neglected to train their entire managerial staff to manage for quality, quality planning, quality control, and quality improvement. Lacking such training and experience, they were seriously hindered, and the quality goals remained as a wish list.

Many companies refused to use self-directed teams. They may have trained empowered workers, but those same workers were not allowed to supervise processes. Unsuccessful organizations also resisted partnerships with suppliers. They missed the revolution in supplier relations and remained adversaries. They were not willing to share information or participate in joint planning and improvement projects. Unsuccessful companies did not thoroughly look at business-process quality management. During the 1980s there emerged a new finding: Many quality problems were traceable to business processes rather than to factory processes.

Deming-Juran Rivalry

For more than four decades, Deming and Juran have been the preeminent champions of quality. Although they cross paths often and maintain an air of cordiality, beneath the surface they are keen rivals.

Deming, the senior guru of statistical quality control (SQC), towers over Juran in both physical stature and fame. He is, after all, the namesake of Japan's Deming Prize. It was created in 1951, just after his first lecture tour there, and quickly became Japan's most coveted industrial award. Still a spry workaholic at 91, Deming has a legendary caustic temper that flares at the suggestion that Juran's ideas have much merit or staying power.

Along with his trademark BMW tie, Juran is best known for being the elder diplomat of total quality control (TQC). He too has found his most loyal following in Japan, where he first described his method in 1954. While Deming's three-year lead there has won him more notice, many people feel that Juran's influence has been greater over the years. In 1969, acknowledging Juran's role, a prestigious prize, the Juran Medal, was created to match the Deming Prize.

Despite their differences, Deming and Juran have lived parallel lives. Both came from humble origins: Deming grew up in a tar paper shack near Cody, Wyoming; Juran in a tar paper shack near Minneapolis, Minnesota. Both got into the quality game by chance.

In the mid-1920s, both men took jobs with the Western Electric Company. Both came under the influence of Walter A. Shewhart, the AT&T Bell Laboratories physicist, who was turning statistical concepts that originated in agricultural research into a manufacturing discipline. After World War II, both Deming and Juran became independent consultants.

Deming still runs a one-man show from a Washington, D.C., office, though he is now surrounded by disciples. Five years ago, he began videotaping selected lectures and conversations with other quality experts. He still attends the "Deming Prize" ceremonies each October in Tokyo.

Juran ended his one-man act in 1979 and founded the Juran Institute to carry on his life's work and build a library of videotapes and training materials. In 1989, he stepped down from the Wilton (Connecticut) institute. He passed the baton—actually, one of his BMW ties—to A. Blanton Godfrey, former head of quality theory at Bell Labs. Now, Juran works mainly at home on the history of management, and on his memoirs of the quality revolution.

For Japan, merely reliable products are no longer good enough. From hand-painted vases to high-tech design and assembly of bike frames, attention to detail is the hallmark of Japanese quality. Japanese auto companies, for example, are aggressively moving away from quality that is taken for granted to quality that fascinates.

In 40 years, a focus on quality has turned Japan from a maker of knickknacks into an economic powerhouse—and U.S. and European companies are being forced to respond. The result: a global revolution affecting every facet of business. Clearly, high quality lowers total costs while improving the products and services. For the 1990s and far beyond, quality must remain the priority for business ("The Quality Imperative" 1991).

At a recent conference in Tokyo, Juran made a rare prediction. Surveying an audience of mostly Japanese executives who have used his quality control methods to humble their U.S. competitors, he declared that America is about to bounce back. In the 1990s, he said "Made in the U.S.A." will become a symbol of world-class quality again. Even if the U.S. does not catch up with Japan, he expects big gains in competitiveness. "When 30 percent of U.S. products were failures versus 3 percent for Japan, it is an enormous difference. But at failures of 0.3 percent and .03 percent, it would be difficult for anyone to tell" ("The Quality Imperative" 1991, p. 8). It remains to be seen if Juran's vision will be fulfilled.

Major industries in the United States and Europe are decided to prove him right. These awakened giants see an urgent need to match the close-to-perfection standard set by Japan after 40 years of dogged effort. Catching up with Japan may be almost incidental to the mere effort of trying that will, in many ways, change the way business is done.

Already, business schools are revamping their MBA programs to reflect their new thrust. One after another, U.S. companies are establishing an office called "Vice-President for Quality." Gross deficiencies discovered by the four-year-old Baldrige Quality Award competition, a response to Japan's 40-year-old Deming Prize, are being taken to heart. There is now widespread realization that quality is simply not implicit in the way U.S. companies design and make products, or in the way they treat customers.

An ironic sign is that the focus on quality is transcending an us-versus-them mentality. Here and there, a new philosophy is taking hold: Excellence should be the norm, not the exception. Motorola, Inc. for example, may soon adopt an unheard-of goal—60 defects for every billion components it makes.

It's not that quality is hard to define: it's simply the absence of variation. Thus, a Chevrolet can have just as much quality as a Rolls-Royce, and the service at a discount store can be equally as "good"—free of variations—as at Bergdorf-Goodman.

Trade barriers include: (1) tariffs, (2) quotas, (3) voluntary restraints, (4) boycotts, (5) monetary barriers (differential exchange rates, approval requirements for foreign exchange of imports), and (6) standards in health, safety, and product qualities.

As trade barriers come down, worldwide competition will intensify. Only companies with the finest quality will thrive—but not because of quality alone ("The Quality Imperative" 1991). Two by-products of making or doing things better are usually lower costs and higher productivity.

Until recently, many such efforts were delayed by the mistaken belief that better quality costs more. Because excellence is measured by lack of defects, "the historical approach was to add more inspection steps," says John C. Day, DuPont Company's manager of world-class manufacturing. In an inspection-oriented plant, more than half of all workers are somehow involved in finding and reworking rejects. The total investment in this process can account for 20 percent to 35 percent of production costs, and in extreme cases, 50 percent.

The Japanese, following the advice of Deming and Juran, devised a cheaper system. They inspect a product before it is made—in the design stage—and they engineer the manufacturing process to be stable and reliable. If the design and the process are solid, quality is inherent.

In the United States, SQC was widely used during World War II. After the war, companies were too busy to bother. Swamped by sudden demand, they cranked out products and let quality fend for itself.

The Japanese, meanwhile, were getting ahead. They bought into Juran's idea of total quality control and applied quality principles to every operation, including their dealings with suppliers. Consequently, Toyota Motor Company Vice-President, Taichi Ohno, and industrial consultant Shiego Shingo devised Toyota's Kanban system, which blossomed into the just-in-time (JIT) movement. The idea behind JIT is delivering parts to an assembly line at just the moment they are needed. This holds down costs, but it requires consistently high quality throughout the supply chain ("The Quality Imperative" 1991).

Feigenbaum

Armand Feigenbaum, then head of Quality Control at General Electric, argued for a systematic and total approach to quality. He wanted the involvement of all functions in the quality process. Otherwise, Feigenbaum (1983) claimed, quality would be inspected and controlled after the fact and not built in at an early stage.

Interestingly, these American leaders have significantly contributed to the highly successful Japanese quality movement. Together, Juran and Feigenbaum awakened the Japanese to the less statistical aspects of quality management.

STATISTICAL QUALITY CONTROL

The true test of any product is its ability to meet the needs of its user. Indeed, many authors define quality as "fitness for use" (Montgomery 1991). There are two generally recognized aspects of quality: quality of design and quality of conformance. Quality of design refers to the type of product to be made, the design of the product, and the production process. Quality of conformance refers to the uniformity of the product and how well it conforms to the specifications required by the design. The field of statistical process control (SPC) is concerned with achieving higher levels in quality of conformance. Higher levels of conformance leads to many benefits, including increased productivity through greater yields and decreased costs through reductions in inspection, scrap, and rework.

If a product is to consistently meet the customers' needs it should be produced by a stable process. A stable process is better able to meet the customer's need for a uniform, high-quality product. The aim of SPC is process stability through the reduction of process variability. This is done by distinguishing between *common cause variation* and *special cause variation*. Common causes are small, uncontrollable influences that are an inherent part of the process. They cannot be removed from the process without inducing basic changes in the process that usually require management action. Special causes are larger, unusual influences that can be removed from the process. Variability in raw materials, operator errors, or improperly adjusted machines are some examples of special cause variability. A process that is operating with only common cause variability present is said to be in-statistical-control. The control chart is but one tool in the quest for variability reduction. It is used to decide whether a process is in-control.

The control chart occupies a prominent place in the effort toward increased product quality in industry today. Traditional control charts, such as the Shewhart, Cumulative Sum (CUSUM), and Exponentially Weighted Moving Average (EWMA) charts, are used to monitor production processes; their purpose is to identify the causes of process variation. These control charts are based on summary statistics obtained from samples of data that are plotted against time. The summary statistics are compared to predetermined critical values called control limits. Points that exceed the control limits or exhibit nonrandom patterns are an indication that the process is out-of-control and in need of adjustment.

THE SHEWHART CONTROL CHART

The control chart was developed by Walter Shewhart at Bell Telephone Laboratories. It consists of a graphical display of a numerical quality characteristic obtained from samples of observations and plotted against the time order in which the samples were taken. In the typical application of the Shewhart control chart, random samples of observations are collected on the quality characteristic of concern. Sample averages, and a measure of sample dispersion (either the sample range, R, or the sample standard deviation, S) are calculated for each sample.

Under the assumption that the observations, X_i, are independent and normally distributed with mean and standard deviation, denoted by $X_i \sim iidN \ (\mu, \sigma)$, the sample means are also independent and distributed as $N(\mu, \sigma/n)$. Defining X_{ij} as the jth observation in the ith sample of size n, the sample mean, sample range, and sample standard deviation are represented by

$$\bar{X}_i = \frac{1}{n} \sum_{j=1}^{n} X_{ij} \tag{6.1}$$

$$R_i = \max_j X_{ij} - \min_j X_{ij}, \ n \geqslant 2 \tag{6.2}$$

and

$$S_i = \left[\frac{1}{n-1} \sum_{j=1}^{n} (X_{ij} - \bar{X}_i)^2 \right]^{1/2} \tag{6.3}$$

for $i = 1, 2, \ldots, m$ and $j = 1, 2, \ldots, n$.

Since the mean and the standard deviation are usually unknown, they are estimated. The mean μ is typically estimated by $\bar{\bar{X}}$, given by

$$\bar{\bar{X}} = \frac{1}{m} \sum_{i=1}^{m} \bar{X}_i. \tag{6.4}$$

The standard deviation is approximated using

$$\bar{R} = \sum_{i=1}^{m} R_i \ / m \tag{6.5}$$

or

$$\bar{S} = \sum_{i=1}^{m} S_i \ / m \tag{6.6}$$

by letting

$$\hat{\sigma} = \overline{R}/d_2 \text{ or } \hat{\sigma} = \overline{S}/c_4. \tag{6.7}$$

The values of d_2 and c_4 are constants that render an unbiased estimate of the process standard deviation. Tabled values of d_2 and c_4 are documented (Montgomery 1991).

A Shewhart control chart consists of a plot of sample means (equation 6.1) plotted against time. The plotted values are compared to reference values called control limits. The control limits are typically determined by

$$\overline{\overline{X}} \pm k\hat{\sigma}/\sqrt{n} \tag{6.8}$$

where k is a constant selected to achieve a desired in-control ARL. Typically k is set equal to three to achieve an in-control ARL of 370 resulting in control limits of

$$\overline{\overline{X}} \pm 3\frac{\overline{R}}{d_2\sqrt{n}} \text{ or } \overline{\overline{X}} \pm 3\frac{\overline{S}}{c_4\sqrt{n}}. \tag{6.9}$$

The process is allowed to run uninterrupted as long as the plotted values fall within the control limits. A signal occurs when an observed value exceeds these limits.

The Individuals control chart is a special case of the Shewhart control chart whereby each sample consists of a single observation. Defining the ith moving range to be

$$MR_i = |X_i - X_{i-1}|, i = 2, 3, \ldots, m \tag{6.10}$$

and

$$\overline{MR} = \frac{1}{m-1} \sum_{i=2}^{m} MR_i \tag{6.11}$$

the control limits are

$$\overline{X} \pm k\overline{MR}/d_2 \text{ or } \overline{X} \pm kS/c_4 \tag{6.12}$$

where S is the sample standard deviation of all the observations. The formulation of control limits based on S (equation 6.12) is not recommended because it can result in inflated control limits and undesirable statistical properties for the Individuals control chart.

Table 6.1 shows a set of observations from a normal distribution with mean 0 and standard deviation 1. At time period 21, the mean shifted from 0 to 1.5. A Shewhart (Individuals) control chart on these data is displayed in Figure 6.1.

Table 6.1
Observations from an N(0,1) Distribution with a Shift of Size 1.5 in the Mean at Observation 21

TIME PERIOD i	X_i
1	-0.8826
2	0.6375
3	-2.5821
4	0.3677
5	1.4422
6	0.7892
7	-0.2877
8	2.0919
9	0.9169
10	-0.2966
11	-1.2153
12	0.3054
13	0.0808
14	-0.2172
15	-0.6937
16	-0.3141
17	-0.3084
18	0.4050
19	0.8858
20	0.9366
21	1.3072
22	1.4625
23	0.9896
24	2.2706
25	2.5073
26	2.3921
27	2.0165
28	0.8253
29	1.7077
30	1.7109

The control limits were set equal to 2.88 to achieve an in-control ARL of 250. Observations 1–30 all fall within the control limits. The absence of a signal here is indicative of the Shewhart control chart's insensitivity to small process shifts based on these limits.

The primary criticism of the Shewhart control chart has been its insensitivity to small shifts in process mean. Supplementary runs rules (Western Electric's *Statistical Quality Control Handbook 1956*, pp. 149–183) have been recommended to counteract this shortcoming (Champ and Woodall 1987). Runs rules

Figure 6.1
Shewhart (Individuals) Control Chart (Shift at $i = 21$)

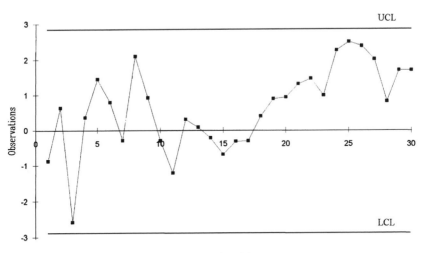

Time Period, i

are essentially attempts at detecting nonrandom patterns on the Shewhart control chart that may suggest small shifts in the mean. These rules are strictly applicable only in monitoring independent statistics (like the sample mean, $_l$, on the Shewhart control chart) because correlated statistics may induce nonrandom patterns that violate the runs rules. The rules suggest that a process is out-of-control if:

1. One point exceeds the 3 control limits.
2. Two out of three consecutive points fall on the same side of the center line and beyond the 2 limits from the center line.
3. Four out of five consecutive points fall on the same side of the center line and beyond the 1 limits from the center line.
4. Eight consecutive points fall on one side of the center line. Based on runs rules (2) or (4), a signal occurs at observation 25 on Figure 6.1.

THE CUMULATIVE SUM (CUSUM) CONTROL CHART

The Cumulative Sum (CUSUM) control chart is an alternative to the Shewhart control chart that is particularly useful in detecting small shifts in the process mean (Montgomery 1991, p. 279). The CUSUM control chart can be represented by a series of cumulative statistics monitored by V-mask control limits or, equivalently, by using two one-sided cumulative sums.

The V-mask form of the CUSUM control chart consists of the statistics

Figure 6.2
V-Mask CUSUM Control Chart (Shift at i = 21) with d = 4.1 and θ = 20.55

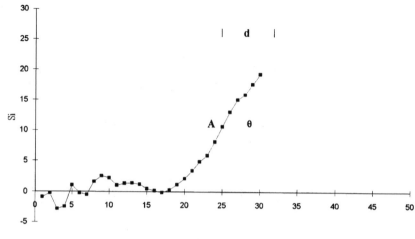

$$S_i = \sum_{j=1}^{i} (\overline{X}_j - \mu), \ i = 1, 2, \ldots \tag{6.13}$$

plotted against the sample number i, where $\overline{X}_j$ is the sample mean for the jth sample and μ is the target for the process mean. Figure 6.2 displays the V-mask CUSUM control chart for the data of Table 6.1 using μ = 0 and σ = 1. The point A of the V-mask is placed on the most recent S'_i. The angles of each arm from the horizontal and the lead distance, d, are used in the V-mask construction. If any of the previous cumulative sum statistics, $S'_1, S'_2, \ldots, S'_{i-1}$, falls outside the arms of the V-mask, the process mean is assumed to have shifted. The slope of the sequence of observations over a specified time period measures the average deviation from the target. It is often suggested that a scaling factor be used so that a distance of one unit on the horizontal axis corresponds to a distance of $w = 2\sigma/n$ units on the vertical axis when drawing the V-mask limits.

The V-mask representation of the CUSUM control chart is not favored for the following reasons:

1. The cumulative sums, S'_i, can wander significantly, even if the process mean is on target.

2. It is unclear how much historical information must be retained.

3. The V-mask must be plotted for each data point. For these reasons, the two-sided CUSUM representation is used in this study.

The mathematically equivalent two-sided CUSUM control chart, also called a tabular CUSUM control chart, requires calculating,

$$S_i = \max[0, (\overline{X}_i - \mu_o)/S_{\overline{X}} - K + S_{i-1}] \qquad (6.14)$$

$$T_i = \min[0, (\overline{X}_i - \mu_o)/S_{\overline{X}} + K + T_{i-1}] \qquad (6.15)$$

where $S_0 = T_0 = 0$ and μ_o is the target value. The reference value K is usually set to $/2$, where θ is the smallest shift in the mean (measured in standard errors) considered important to be detected quickly. If $S_i > h$ or $T_i < -h$ (where h is a critical value), the control chart signals. The value of h is typically set to 4 or 5. Head start values, $S_0 = h/2$ and $T_0 = -h/2$, are recommended for earlier detection of out-of-control situations (Lucas and Crosier 1982). The Shewhart control chart is a special case of the CUSUM control chart with $K = 3\sigma/\sqrt{n}$ and $h = 0$. The two-sided CUSUM control chart is equivalent to the V-mask CUSUM control chart when $K = w \tan\theta$ and $h = wd \tan\theta$.

Table 6.2 shows the two-sided CUSUM statistics for the data set of Table 6.1, with K set equal to 0.75. At time period 21, the mean shifted from 0 to 1.5. A CUSUM control chart on these data is displayed in Figure 6.3. The control limits were set equal to 4.4 to achieve an in-control ARL of 250. For this set of data, observations 1–24 fall within the control limits. Observation 25 exceeds the upper control limit, producing a signal. Although the CUSUM control chart is superior to the Shewhart control chart for detecting small shifts, it is less effective in detecting large shifts in the process mean.

The design of the CUSUM control chart has historically been based on the method of N. L. Johnson (1961). However, Johnson's method performs poorly (Adams et al. 1993). More recently, an alternative design on which the chart might be based has been offered (Woodall and Adams 1993).

THE EXPONENTIALLY WEIGHTED MOVING AVERAGE (EWMA) CONTROL CHART

A third monitoring tool that is useful in detecting small shifts in the process mean is the Exponentially Weighted Moving Average (EWMA) control chart, also known as a Geometric Moving Average (Roberts 1959). The EWMA control chart is based on the statistic

$$Z_i = \lambda \overline{X}_i + (1 - \lambda)Z_{i-1}, \ i = 1, 2, \ldots \qquad (6.16)$$

Table 6.2
CUSUM Statistics with a Shift of Size 1.5 in the Mean at Observation 21 and
$K = 0.75$

TIME PERIOD i	X_i	S_i	T_i
1	-0.8826	0.0000	-0.1326
2	0.6375	0.0000	0.0000
3	-2.5821	0.0000	-1.8321
4	0.3677	0.0000	-0.7144
5	1.4422	0.6922	0.0000
6	0.7892	0.7314	0.0000
7	-0.2877	0.0000	0.0000
8	2.0919	1.3419	0.0000
9	0.9169	1.5088	0.0000
10	-0.2966	0.4622	0.0000
11	-1.2153	0.0000	-0.4653
12	0.3054	0.0000	0.0000
13	0.0808	0.0000	0.0000
14	-0.2172	0.0000	0.0000
15	-0.6937	0.0000	0.0000
16	-0.3141	0.0000	0.0000
17	-0.3084	0.0000	0.0000
18	0.4050	0.0000	0.0000
19	0.8858	0.1358	0.0000
20	0.9366	0.3224	0.0000
21	1.3072	0.8795	0.0000
22	1.4625	1.5921	0.0000
23	0.9896	1.8317	0.0000
24	2.2706	3.3523	0.0000
25	2.5073	5.1096	0.0000
26	2.3921	5.7517	0.0000
27	2.0165	7.0182	0.0000
28	0.8253	7.0935	0.0000
29	1.7077	8.0512	0.0000
30	1.7109	9.0121	0.0000

where λ $(0 < \lambda \leq 1)$ is a smoothing constant. The starting value, Z_o, is typically set to $\overline{\overline{X}}$. Assuming that the process is in-control, then

$$\sigma^2_{Zi} = \frac{\sigma^2}{n} \frac{\lambda}{2 - \lambda} [1 - (1 - \lambda)^{2i}] \qquad (6.17)$$

and control limits are set at $\overline{\overline{X}} \pm c\sigma_{Zi}$. The constant c is selected to achieve a desired in-control ARL.

Figure 6.3
Two-Sided CUSUM Control Chart (Shift at i = 21) with *K* = 0.75 and *h* = 4.4

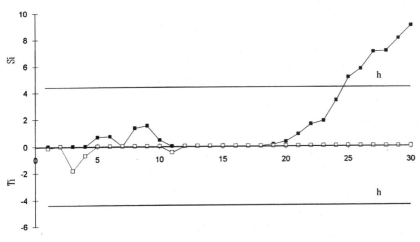

Time Period, i

Larger values of λ give more weight to the present sample. Values of λ in the interval $0.05 \leq \lambda \leq 0.25$ have been recommended with smaller values of λ being more useful in detecting smaller shifts (Montgomery 1991). Note if $\lambda = 1$, the EWMA control chart is equivalent to a Shewhart control chart.

Table 6.3 shows the EWMA statistics for the data set of Table 6.1 with λ set equal to 0.10. At time period 21, the mean shifted from 0 to 1.5. An EWMA control chart is displayed in Figure 6.4. The control limits were set equal to 0.588 to achieve an in-control ARL of 250. Observations 1–23 fall within the control limits. Observation 24 falls above the upper control limit resulting in a signal.

For independent observations, the CUSUM and EWMA control charts are the preferred tools for detecting small shifts in the process mean based on ARLs. Larger shifts are detected more quickly by the Shewhart control chart.

CONCLUSION

To conclude, successful CEOs increasingly use the following sequence in managing quality issues. First, they establish the vision and policies; second, they train the hierarchy; third, they establish the goals to be met; next, they plan the steps to reach the goals and provide the resources. The final phase in the sequence should be to manage and measure quality as seriously as profitability.

Table 6.3
EWMA Statistics with a Shift of Size 1.5 in the Mean at Observation 21 and $\lambda = 0.10$

TIME PERIOD i	X_i	Z_i
1	-0.8826	-0.0883
2	0.6375	-0.0157
3	-2.5821	-0.2723
4	0.3677	-0.2083
5	1.4422	-0.0641
6	0.7892	0.0212
7	-0.2877	-0.0097
8	2.0919	0.2005
9	0.9169	0.2721
10	-0.2966	0.2153
11	-1.2153	0.0722
12	0.3054	0.0955
13	0.0808	0.0941
14	-0.2172	0.0629
15	-0.6937	-0.0127
16	-0.3141	-0.0429
17	-0.3084	-0.0694
18	0.4050	-0.0220
19	0.8858	0.0688
20	0.9366	0.1556
21	1.3072	0.2707
22	1.4625	0.3899
23	0.9896	0.4499
24	2.2706	0.6320
25	2.5073	0.8195
26	2.3921	0.9768
27	2.0165	1.0807
28	0.8253	1.0552
29	1.7077	1.1204
30	1.7109	1.1795

Figure 6.4
EWMA Control Chart (Shift at $i = 21$) with $\lambda = 0.10$

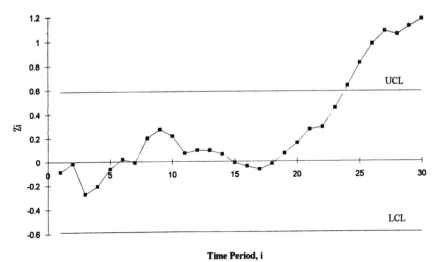

Time Period, i

7

Global Consumers

Niren M. Vyas and Allan C. Reddy

This chapter portrays the salient features of a global consumer. Such a portrayal helps marketers launch major global campaigns or effectively manage their existing global marketing operations. "World economy," "global village," and "spaceship earth" are all terms commonly used by politicians, economists, and business executives today. These terms signify our international interdependence.

GROWTH OF WORLD TRADE

The importance of world trade is recognized by the global community. In the past, trade was conducted internationally, but not at a level—or with the intensity—that it has now achieved. In the last two decades, world trade has expanded from a mere $200 billion to more than $4 trillion. Countries that had never been considered major participants in world trade have suddenly become major economic powers. The concept and understanding of *global consumer*, therefore, have become critical to the success of international companies.

CONTRIBUTING FACTORS

Several factors have contributed to the phenomenal growth in world trade during the last several years. Tariff barriers have come down and continue falling. Successive rounds of bilateral and multinational agreements, such as the General Agreement on Tariffs and Trade (GATT), have lowered tariffs markedly since World War II. Also, regional economic agreements, such as the European Union and the North American Free Trade Agreement (NAFTA), have facilitated trade relations and have further reduced international trade barriers; sometimes they have totally eliminated barriers among member countries. The Iron

Curtain has disintegrated. The Eastern European countries, including former Soviet Union countries, have embraced democracy and free-market economy. The most populous countries of the world, China and India, have opened their markets for international products. These events have given a tremendous boost to world trade.

Worldwide consumer education and awareness expanded because of telecommunications, increased travel, and sundry information sources (electronic and print media) readily available through a variety of products and services. These factors contributed to increased consumer demands worldwide.

Rapid technological growth is greatly influencing consumer markets. Technology is not only reshaping industries but also contributing to market homogenization. Transportation costs have decreased with the use of containerization and larger capacity ships. Increasing ease of communications and data transfer makes it feasible to link operations in different countries. Technology leads to an easy flow of information among buyers, making them aware of new products and thus creating demand. Electronic innovations permit the development of more compact, lighter-weight products that are less expensive to ship.

There is a growing similarity of lifestyles among consumers in various countries. The middle-class segment of the population in industrial, as well as in developing nations, desires similar amenities and lifestyles. Commonality of infrastructure, distribution channels, and marketing approaches has made more and more products and brands available everywhere. This promotes similar buyer needs in different countries. Large retail chains, television advertising, and credit cards are just a few examples of once-isolated phenomena that are rapidly becoming universal.

Global Markets

The markets for goods, services, capital, technology, and even labor are becoming global. Companies can sell products, raise capital, set up research and development centers, hire executives, and provide consulting services in different countries. It is in this sense that the markets are becoming global. As more and more products and services are traded among countries, the more global the market becomes. The more global the market becomes, the more products and services are exchanged—thus creating global consumers.

The Role of Multinational Corporations

The multinational corporations (MNCs), such as Coca-Cola and IBM, play a pivotal role in the expansion of business on an international scale. In the past twenty-five years, they have become the most formidable single factor in world trade and investment. The MNCs play a critical role in the allocation and use of the world's resources by creating new products and services, by stimulating demand for them, and by developing new techniques of manufacturing and distribution worldwide. Current rates of energy consumption, for example, could not be achieved without the contribution of MNCs in the development and expansion of the automotive industry and the production of electrical appliances.

Indeed, the MNCs, characterized by a global strategy of investment, production, and distribution, represent the highest level of participation in international business. According to an estimate by the United Nations, at least 37,000 MNCs were in operation in the early 1990s, controlling more than 200,000 foreign affiliates ("U.N. Report" 1993, p. 1). At the end of 1993, worldwide assets accumulated from past foreign direct investment by these MNCs reached $2.1 trillion. The largest 100 MNCs controlled more than 60 percent of these assets and accounted for about 30 percent of all new foreign direct investment in 1993. Many of these large companies have invested in specific industries. For example, 26 percent of their foreign assets were in electronics, followed by petroleum and mining (24 percent), motor vehicles (19 percent), and chemicals and pharmaceuticals (15 percent).

Most of the MNCs are predominantly large firms. Typically an MNC's annual sales amount to hundreds of millions of dollars. In fact, more than 500 MNCs have annual sales of more than $1 billion. The largest 80 MNCs have sales ranging between $10 billion and $125 billion. Many MNCs derive a substantial portion of their net income and sales from international operations. Several MNCs have a higher annual revenue than the Gross National Product (GNP) of various countries. For example, General Motors ($138.2 billion in sales) generates more revenue annually than the 1993 GNP of Denmark, Greece, or Colombia. Similarly IBM's annual sales ($62.7 billion in 1993) exceed the GNP of New Zealand or Singapore for that year.

MNCs dominate international markets with their technological skills, specialization in specific products or services, and their ability to differentiate their offerings through advertising and promotional efforts. Most MNCs have a sizable number of foreign branches and affiliates. Two hundred MNCs, among the largest in the world, have affiliates in 25 or more countries.

Multinational companies are mainly from industrialized countries. However, their world market share and relative predominance have changed in the last fifteen years. For example, Japanese and Western European companies have gained relative importance, while the U.S. companies to some extent have lost their predominance in the international arena. The biggest contribution of the MNCs is the successful marketing of global brands and creating demand for them.

EXPERIENTIAL DATA

The remainder of the chapter discusses data collected by the authors during their travels to various countries over the past five years. The following countries were visited during this time frame:

1. South Africa, Zimbabwe, Zambia, Kenya, Tanzania, Uganda.

2. Turkey, Greece, Egypt, Morocco, Spain, Portugal.

3. Denmark, Sweden, Norway, Finland.

4. England, Germany, France, Austria, Switzerland, Italy, the Netherlands.

5. Russia, the Czech Republic, Slovakia, Hungary, Poland.

6. Canada, Mexico, Costa Rica, Panama, Ecuador, Argentina, Chile, Paraguay, Brazil.

7. China, Nepal, India, Indonesia, Thailand, Cambodia, Sri Lanka.

8. Taiwan, South Korea, Singapore, Hong Kong, Malaysia, Australia, New Zealand, Fiji.

LIVING STANDARDS WORLDWIDE

Except for Russia and Cambodia, we were able to stay at franchise or chain hotels, such as Sheraton, Hilton, Hyatt, Holiday Inn, Best Western, Radisson, Ramada Inn, Choice hotels, Days Inn, Novotel (French chain) or Swissotel (Swiss chain).

These hotels have a variety of restaurants with Western and international foods. They also have several bars that offer an array of well-known alcoholic and nonalcoholic beverages. They include Coke, Pepsi, Canada Dry, club sodas, European and U.S. brands of mineral waters, and many varieties of international brands of beers and wines. Other alcoholic drinks available are Scotch whiskeys, U.S. bourbons, and many varieties of liquors. Besides restaurants and bars, the majority of these hotels also have several gift shops that carry local souvenirs and international name-brand products. These shops sell a wide selection of international newspapers and magazines in various languages.

The restaurants, bars, and gift shops are visited by local residents of the country, who are familiar with international foods and products. Such familiarity creates demand for these offerings and helps establish channels of distribution in the various countries. For example, Coke, Pepsi-Cola, or both were available in practically all the countries visited. These two soft-drink giants spend several hundred million dollars worldwide in advertising and promotion to establish a brand image. Their billboards on roads, highways, trains, and buses are common sights.

Fast-food franchise operations, such as McDonald's, Burger King, Pizza Hut, Domino's, Hardee's, Kentucky Fried Chicken, International House of Pancakes, Subway, Taco Bell, and Baskin-Robbins were also found in the countries visited. McDonald's, Pizza Hut, and Kentucky Fried Chicken restaurants are a familiar sight even in Moscow, Beijing, and New Delhi. The management and staff of franchise operators are trained by the parent company. Several of the franchise operators visit the franchise headquarters in the United States or Western Europe, thus acquainting themselves with products and services of multinational companies. U.S. car rental companies, such as Hertz, Avis, and National, and several European companies offer their services throughout the Western and

Eastern European countries, Central and South America, Australia, New Zealand, South Africa, and Turkey. The majority of automobiles, buses, motorbikes, and trucks in the countries toured were models from well-known U.S., European, or Japanese manufacturers, although often locally manufactured or assembled. Russia and some Eastern European countries were exceptions; several local brands of cars were observed.

The entertainment industry appears to be internationalized to the maximum extent. American movies and television programs are beamed to all the countries visited. Several television programs are dubbed in the local language. The Cable News Network or its affiliates relay programs regularly to these countries and have large viewing audiences. Multinational companies advertise their brands regularly on television and in movie theaters, creating a tremendous amount of brand awareness for their products and services.

Western music is enjoyed and revered by teenagers and college students. Music videos, audiotapes, and compact discs are available in practically all the countries. We observed these students dancing to Western music in the night-clubs of Cairo, Istanbul, and Kathmandu. Most of these students recognize the famous singers and performers from the United States and Europe. There is tremendous demand for music videos, audiotapes, compact discs, movie video-cassettes, and name-brand musical instruments in these countries. We observed that two teenagers from different lands had much in common in terms of tastes and aspirations. This is the most encouraging sign of nations becoming a global village.

Another stunning observation was the way this young generation (aged 15 through 25) dressed. We visited several university campuses in various countries. Observing the way they dressed, it was difficult to distinguish whether they were on the campus of a U.S. university or on a campus in Kenya. They were in jeans, T-shirts, and tennis shoes or sneakers. They were not dressed in customary local costumes. Several of them were observed wearing famous designer brands: Levi's jeans, polo shirts, and Reebok, Adidas, or Nike shoes. They also desired famous brands of jogging suits, caps, sweaters, sweatshirts, and pullovers. The demand for these products makes it easy for multinational companies to establish effective channels of distribution.

Prestigious sporting events, such as tennis and golf tournaments, soccer championship games, Super Bowl football games, cricket matches (among Commonwealth countries), and Olympic games have worldwide audiences. Other programs, such as beauty pageants and the Oscar Awards ceremony, also attract large viewing audiences globally; and the advertising messages during these events and programs create global awareness.

While on various university campuses, we noticed students using textbooks—especially in business, sciences, engineering, and medicine—written by U.S. and Western European professors. The presence of exchange students and faculty members on these campuses also adds to awareness about global products and generates subtle demand from the local population. Several U.S. and Western

European universities have alliances with universities in other parts of the world to exchange knowledge and global issues. One of the biggest fascinations for foreign students is to attend a United States or Western European university; the parents of some these students indicated a similar desire—to have their children educated in prestigious United States or Western European universities.

Expansion of operations by MNCs in various parts of the world and opening offices beyond the United States and Europe by organizations such as the United Nations, GATT, the World Bank, and the International Monetary Fund give impetus to world travel. In addition, several thousand technical, social, educational, scientific, and business conferences are held globally. In the past few years, world travel has increased at the rate of 6 percent—the majority of which is done by air. The food, drinks, and snacks served on international flights; the newspapers, magazines, music, and entertainment provided; and the duty-free products available during flights and at international airports have all contributed to the term *global consumer*, those who have or desire common products and lifestyles. The living standards in developing countries are rising. We have witnessed this firsthand. Household electrical and electronic appliances, considered luxury items a few years ago, have become needed products in many homes. Refrigerators, ceiling fans, ovens, toasters, mixers, radios, TV sets, washing machines, and so forth have become required appliances for middle-class families in developing countries, and multinational companies are rushing to address these needs. Electronic items, such as tape and CD players, VCRs, cameras, and camcorders, are purchased by upper-middle-class families. It is common, however, to find a VCR in operation even in some slum dwellings of Bombay, Bangkok, and Panama. Toshiba, Panasonic, Sony, Samsung, Casio, Philips, and General Electric are globally recognized names. Developing countries are flooded with billboards and posters displaying these companies' products. With respect to cigarettes, American brands, such as Camel and Marlboro, and such European brands as 555 and Dunhill, are advertised and sold extensively.

Name-brand household products occupied premium shelf space in many of the shops we visited. The products ranged from Ivory soap, Colgate toothpaste, Lipton tea, and Oil of Olay to several brand-name cosmetics, perfumes, shampoos, detergents, coffees, canned fruits, and vegetables. Frito-Lay corn chips, Pringles potato chips, and Planters peanuts were the most common snack food varieties found in international markets. Other food items included Kraft products, Nestlé products (baby formulas), Gerber baby food products, Hershey's chocolate bars, Wrigley's gums, Kellogg's cereals, and Cadbury's candies. Several additional products stand out in brand awareness and advertisements: Gillette (shaving cream, blades, and razors), Singer (sewing machines), Parker (pens), Black & Decker (tools), and Goodyear (tires).

The most striking observation concerned the commonality of pharmaceutical products available across the various countries. Several newspaper articles suggested the exorbitant amount of price differential that existed for prescription drugs—especially between developed and developing countries. One of the authors ran out of his prescription drugs in Rio de Janeiro, Brazil. He requested a drugstore employee to provide the needed medicine without a prescription as a special case because he was a foreign visitor, and he left the prescription at home. The author was astonished that medicine in Brazil was available without a doctor's prescription, and the price was one-fifth the cost of the same medicine in the United States. There are only about a dozen large pharmaceutical companies in the world: Merk, Bristol-Myers, Squibb, Ciba-Geigey, Glaxo, Schering, Parke-Davis, Pfizer, Searle, and Upjohn, to name a few.

In the 1970s, developing a new drug cost about $16 million and took four to five years. The drug could be produced in Britain or the United States and eventually exported. Today, developing and introducing a new drug costs about $250 million and takes as long as twelve years. Only a global product for a global market can support that kind of risk.

In all the countries visited, the drugs from major multinational companies were available. The government in many developing countries set the price of the medicine to make it affordable for everyone. Viewed from this perspective, the pharmaceutical companies are promoting a worthy cause by providing medicine to the developing countries at a reasonable cost. The developed countries are subsidizing the cost in developing countries.

Large markets exist in developing countries for cold remedies, aspirin products, and skin care products. According to a recent article in the *Wall Street Journal*, "The so-called emerging markets have already emerged. They are not just booming: they are buying—buying everything from earth movers to cellular phones to soft drinks and cognac from the advanced countries, principally the United States, Western Europe, and Japan." This means the global consumer is emerging in emerging markets.

CONCLUSION

The multinational companies cannot afford to ignore global consumers who live in highly populated countries like China and India. The population of India is about 980 million, but only 6 percent of this population has a buying power equivalent to the buying power of a typical Western European country. This segment, which represents a population of about 59 million people, is larger than the entire population of France. Thus, each country has a segment of population that can be called a global consumer market. This is an exciting, challenging development for MNCs, economic stability, world peace. Should we not use global trade as a tool to uplift the living standards of the world community?

8

Distribution Considerations in Marketing to High-Tech Consumers

Carol C. Bienstock

This chapter presents the dynamics of distribution in marketing to high-tech consumers. It is divided into four sections. The first section discusses environmental factors that significantly impact on a firm's distribution strategy if it seeks to market products to high-tech customers. The second section discusses distribution intensity considerations when marketing to high-tech customers. The third section addresses the role of wholesalers and retailers as distribution channel participants for firms distributing to high-tech customers. The final section summarizes the key issues presented in the chapter.

Generally, channels of distribution for high-tech products operate as shown in Figure 8.1. The characteristics of a firm's products prompt the firm to identify and target "high-tech" customer segments; to attain sales, profitability, and customer-satisfaction goals, the products must be available for customers to purchase. The portion of a firm's marketing strategy that assures customers have access to the firm's products is known as *distribution strategy*, and the institutions (e.g., wholesalers and retailers) that take part in product distribution comprise the *marketing* or *distribution channels* for those products.

Marketing channels are sets of interdependent organizations that are utilized during the development of a new product or service. The distribution tasks undertaken by these interdependent organizations are vital to the success or failure of a firm's product. For example, consider the situation faced by Sony in the mid-1980s. Sony's sales in the northeastern U.S. were disappointing, despite a well-deserved reputation for technically advanced, high-quality consumer electronics products. Management discovered that Sony's products were not achieving adequate retail coverage in this region. To increase their retail presence in the northeast, Sony began distributing their products through a net-

Figure 8.1
Channels of Distribution for High-Tech Products

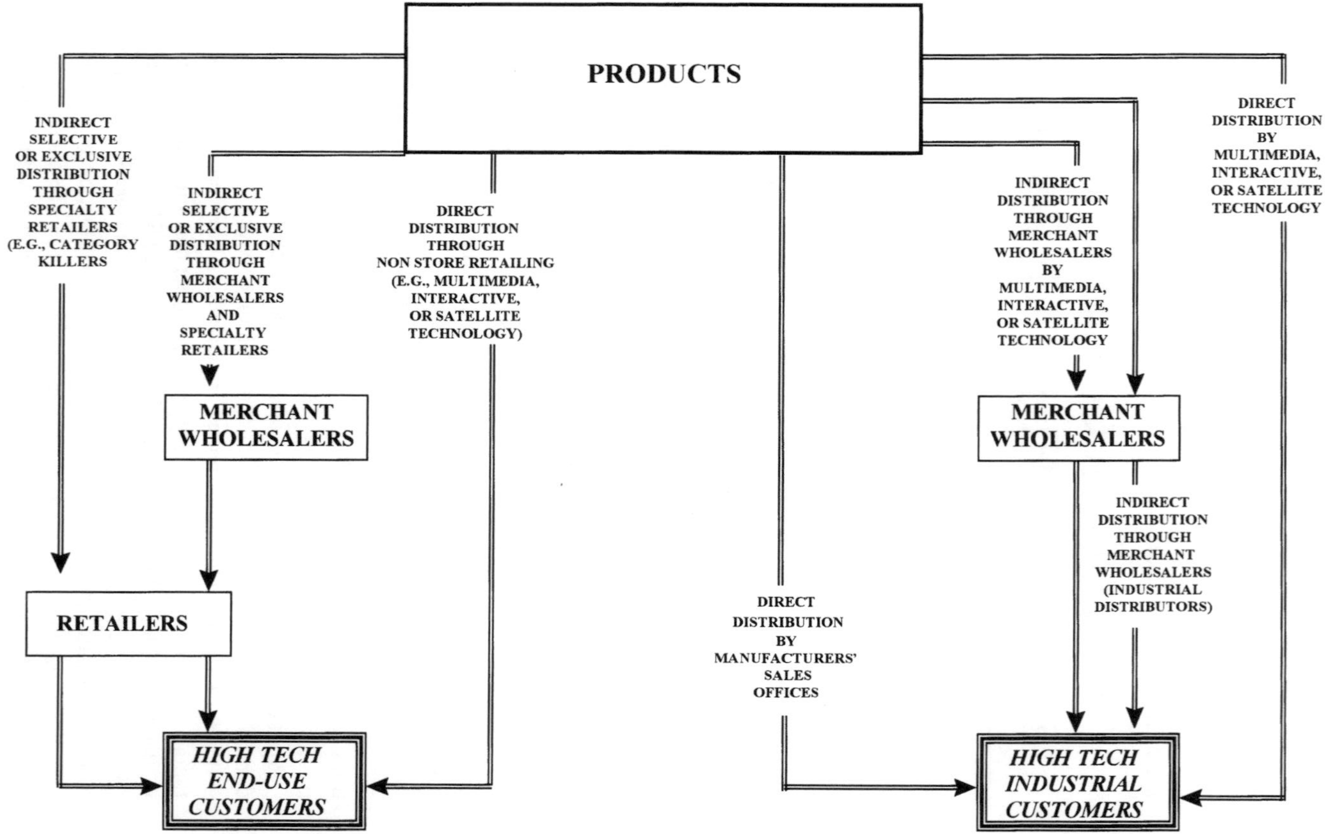

work of wholesalers who, in turn, placed Sony's products with most retailers (Rosenbloom 1991).

Two concepts from economics explain why marketing channels are important to a firm's distribution objectives. The first is specialization and division of labor, and the second is contractual efficiency. The principle of specialization and division of labor advocates the assignment of distribution tasks to firms that possess the necessary expertise. This principle contributes to an understanding of why distribution tasks are often managed interorganizationally, rather than intraorganizationally; that is, why a firm may feel that their distribution strategy can be managed more efficiently and effectively by a group of independent organizations, rather than by managing it themselves.

The second concept, contractual efficiency, focuses on how many contacts must take place between a seller and a buyer for a transaction to be completed. By using channel intermediaries to accomplish distribution tasks, producers can increase their distribution coverage and potential for sales, without having to meet each potential buyer (Rosenbloom 1991). This idea is illustrated in the Sony example above. By relying on a network of wholesalers to contact and distribute its products to retailers, Sony increased the number of retailers that sold its products, without having to contact each retailer itself.

ENVIRONMENTAL FACTORS IMPACTING ON DISTRIBUTION TO HIGH-TECH CUSTOMERS

Usually, there are five major environmental influences of which all firms should be aware when designing distribution strategy and deciding what institutions should constitute their distribution channels. These influences are sociocultural, competitive, legal, technological, and economic (Rosenbloom 1991).

Sociocultural factors tend to influence demand in marketing channels; competitive and legal factors influence supply in marketing channels; and technological and economic factors influence both demand and supply in marketing channels (Stern and El-Ansary 1992). Although all five of these environmental influences are important, for firms marketing products to high-tech customers, it can be argued that the more important influences on distribution strategy are sociocultural and technological.

SOCIOCULTURAL FACTORS

Sociocultural factors influence demand for products because they include social factors (such as roles, family, and reference-group influences), as well as such customer characteristics as demographic traits, lifestyles, cultural values, and attitudes (Kotler 1995; Pride and Ferrell 1995). Although these sociocultural factors have the potential to impact on demand and influence distribution decisions, for firms distributing products to high-tech customers, reference-group influences, along with lifestyles and demographic traits, are likely to be the most significant influences on decisions regarding distribution.

Reference groups are groups that individuals actually belong to (associative groups), aspire to belong to (aspirational groups), or do not wish to be associated with (dissociative groups). Associative reference groups include, for example, the organization that a person works for. Reference groups impact on demand because they shape values, attitudes, and actual behavior. Reference groups affect values, attitudes, and behaviors by exposing members and potential members to new ideas, and by the customers' desire to conform to the attitudes and behaviors of a reference group. (Kotler 1994; Pride and Ferrell 1995). There is evidence that the influence of reference groups on purchasing behavior varies according to the type of product and the life cycle stage of the product. When products are in the introductory stage of the life cycle, purchasing decisions are often influenced by others to a greater degree than purchasing decisions for products in the mature phase of their life cycle (Kotler 1994). Because the types of products that high-tech industrial customers require, or that high-tech end users demand, are frequently in the introductory stage of their life cycle, decisions about distribution strategy should include employing channel intermediaries to target these customers.

Reference groups, particularly associative reference groups, serve important informational purposes by disseminating details about products, especially the technologically complex ones. Much of the information that is available through reference groups originates with, and is distributed by, the *opinion leaders* in the group. Opinion leaders are members of reference groups that, because of their status or role in the group, have a strong influence on the other members of the group (Kotler 1994). Reference-group members who have an interest in high-tech products (members of organizations that use computer hardware and software, for example) and who are knowledgeable about the latest innovations in computer hardware, software, or both function as opinion leaders. These opinion leaders are, therefore, a relevant portion of high-tech-customer market segments. Besides being potential buyers of high-tech products for their personal use, these individuals may also exert considerable influence on industrial purchases of high-tech products through their role as opinion leaders in their organizational reference group.

Effectively reaching these opinion leaders, particularly for organizational purchases, is an important factor to be considered when designing distribution strategy for high-tech products. Channel intermediaries, such as manufacturers' agents or sales representatives for industrial distributors, must be aware of the potential of these high-tech opinion leaders in an organization. Because customers often seek a high level of information when products are new or technically complex (Stern et al. 1996), manufacturers' agents, sales representatives, and retail sellers should structure their sales presentation and after-sale activities accordingly.

We can describe *lifestyle* as a person's "pattern of living in the world as expressed in the person's activities, interests, and opinions. Lifestyle portrays the 'whole person' interacting with his or her environment'' (Kotler 1994, p. 182). For many years the Stanford Research Institute has been conducting research on identifying lifestyles and combining them with demographic traits into actionable classifications. Its classification system is known as the Values and Lifestyles Framework (VALS and VALS2™). This framework identifies nine lifestyle groups, two of which are of particular interest to firms distributing to high-tech customers. These two groups are identified as *actualizers* and *strivers*.

Actualizers are described as having high incomes and high self-esteem. Furthermore, customers belonging to this lifestyle classification are described as image-conscious, having diverse interests, and being open to change (Kotler 1995; Levy and Weitz 1995). In fact, actualizers are, in many ways, prototypical of the image evoked when one hears the words *high-tech customer*. Strivers, the other lifestyle classification, are described as being status oriented, and having fewer resources (e.g., income) than actualizers, but exhibiting a propensity for emulating reference groups they aspire to join (Kotler 1994; Levy and Weitz 1995).

These two lifestyle classifications are the most likely to contain high-tech customers. Actualizers, with their wide range of interests and openness to change, are highly likely to demand high-tech products. Actualizers have sufficient discretionary income to constitute a viable market segment. Strivers do not possess the level of discretionary income that actualizers do, but they are highly motivated to imitate reference groups to which they aspire to belong. Because both strivers and actualizers are status conscious, actualizers constitute a potential reference group to which strivers might seek to belong; therefore, strivers could also be a market segment that contains high-tech customers. Through research on these lifestyle segments, information about the numbers of each segment that live in geographic areas identified by zip codes, along with what products are bought by the various segments, is available (Levy and Weitz 1995). This information is indispensable to firms distributing to high-tech customers, as they make decisions about the locations of their wholesale and retail intermediaries.

The lifestyle and demographic information on these high-tech-customer segments is also important to firms because it guides their push and pull promotional strategies. Push promotions are aimed at distribution channel members, motivating them to ''push'' the product through the channel to the next level and, finally, to the customer. Push promotions include such activities as cooperative advertising and promotional allowance agreements with channel members; sales contests and incentives; and special promotional deals (e.g., discounts for channel-member purchases of a product during a specified period of time). Pull promotions are directed at end-use customers and are designed to encourage them to request a product from channel members, that is, wholesalers, retailers, or both (Stern et al. 1996). Pull promotions include print and television advertising and sales promotions, such as coupons and rebates (Pride and Ferrell 1995). To adequately manage the push portion of a promotional strategy, a firm must be able to design their promotions appropriately. When push promotions are offered without considering channel members' needs and without understanding what is and is not effective, a high degree of conflict can occur between manufacturers and distribution channel members (Curhan and Kopp 1987). The information provided by lifestyle and demographic analyses can promote a greater understanding of the context within which channel members operate, along with some specific knowledge of channel members' requirements in terms of promotional support. This understanding and appreciation for channel members' circumstances is important for ensuring the success of push promotional strategies. Likewise, lifestyle and demographic analyses facilitate an understanding of the attitudes and motivations of high-tech customers and which promotional outlets are most likely to reach them.

Technological Factors

The technological environment is characterized by an increasing rate of technological change (Kotler 1994), which has obvious implications for product design and development. However, the technological environment has influenced the distribution strategy of firms targeting high-tech customers in two ways. The first of these technological influences derives from the increasing potential for firms to forsee customers demanding information because of advances in information technology.

The second technological influence arises from the opportunities for alternative distribution channels offered by the developments in multimedia, interactive, and satellite technologies. The influence of multimedia, interactive, and satellite technologies will be discussed in the section dealing with the roles of wholesaling and retailing in distribution channels for high-tech customers.

The combination of the Universal Product Code—developed jointly through the efforts of the Grocery Manufacturers of America and the Food Marketing Institute—and laser scanning technology yielded product point-of-purchase information.

The reason that access to customer point-of-purchase information is important is that new technologies increase the potential for new products, as well as cause a compression of product life cycles (Kotler 1994; Rosenbloom 1995). New products, which frequently arise from new technologies and are marketed to sophisticated, that is, high-tech customers, possess no history. This makes it impossible for firms to use past sales records to facilitate sales forecasting for production and physical distribution scheduling. Access to the point-of-purchase information can facilitate more accurate sales forecasts, resulting in product availability and increased sales, profits, and customer satisfaction from potentially profitable high-tech-customer market segments.

DISTRIBUTION-INTENSITY CONSIDERATIONS WHEN MARKETING TO HIGH-TECH CUSTOMERS

When designing distribution channels, firms must decide the distribution intensity at each channel level (e.g., wholesale level or retail level) that will enable them to achieve their distribution objectives. Levels of distribution intensity are described as exclusive, selective, and intensive.

A firm distributing exclusively or selectively distributes through only one channel intermediary (e.g., retailer) in a geographic area (e.g., a city), or through a only a few, selected intermediaries in a geographic area. Intensive distribution describes a situation where a firm distributes a product through every available channel intermediary (e.g., retailer) in a geographic area. For example, convenience products, those items that customers are not willing to expend effort to acquire, must be available in many locations.

Exclusive and selective distribution is used when a firm wants to exert a moderate to large degree of control over product distribution. Because of the desire for distribution control, the working relationship between manufacturers and their exclusive or selective channel members is close. The manufacturer expects the retailer, for example, to be an aggressive and informed product advocate. Exclusive or selective distribution can result in an enhanced product image, which enables both manufacturers and distribution channel members to achieve higher gross margins.

Exclusive or selective distribution provides the high level of product information that even relatively well-informed high-tech customers may want if products are new or technically complex. In addition, the promise of exclusive or selective distribution may also be used to secure channel members for a new product. If a firm is targeting high-tech customers with a new product, the promise of an exclusive or a selective distribution strategy may attract channel members to carry the new product (Kotler 1994; Stern et al. 1996; Rosenbloom 1995).

ROLES OF WHOLESALING AND RETAILING IN DISTRIBUTION CHANNELS FOR HIGH-TECH CUSTOMERS

Wholesalers and retailers are channel intermediaries, occupying positions between manufacturers and customers. Because of the distribution functions that can be performed by wholesalers and retailers, an understanding of their role as potential channel members is essential for firms' distribution of products to high-tech customers.

Wholesaling

A wholesale transaction is a sale to another reseller (another wholesaler or a retailer), or to an industrial or institutional customer for use in their operations

(Stern et al. 1996). Wholesalers occupy an intermediate position in distribution channels, situated below manufacturers and above retailers. According to the 1992 *Census of Wholesale Trade*, there are three principal classifications of wholesalers: merchant wholesalers, agent wholesalers, and manufacturers' sales offices and branches.

The principal difference between merchant wholesalers and agent wholesalers is that merchant wholesalers accept ownership or title to the products they handle, while agent wholesalers do not. A secondary difference is that often, the range of services offered by merchant wholesalers is larger than the range of services offered by agent wholesalers.

Because of the range of distribution tasks they do for multiple manufacturers, merchant wholesalers can frequently do these tasks more efficiently than agent wholesalers (Rosenbloom 1995). Furthermore, if a manufacturer intends to target high-tech customers with a new product, there is obviously an inherent risk involved, both short term and long term, regarding whether sales will materialize. Merchant wholesalers hold product inventory and take title; this is attractive to a manufacturer because, once the product is sold to the merchant wholesaler, the manufacturer can record the transaction as a sale on the income statement.

Another distribution task frequently provided by merchant wholesalers is the maintenance of an outside sales force. These representatives can accomplish sales contacts for a product over a large geographic area, preventing the need for the product manufacturer to maintain an outside sales force (Narus and Anderson 1986). Furthermore, the use of merchant wholesalers' outside sales forces can accomplish the appropriate level of retail distribution intensity (e.g., selective) in a geographical area—without the manufacturer having to contact each retailer.

Merchant wholesalers' outside salespeople can identify high-tech customers and provide product demonstrations and explanations. Merchant wholesalers' outside sales forces can also maintain after-sale customer support services, services that are particularly important when selling new or technically complex products to high-tech industrial customers. Merchant wholesalers further provide a variety of products from different manufacturers (Rosenbloom 1995). This is particularly important for high-tech customers because they are likely to be interested in or require a variety of new technical products.

Manufacturers' sales offices and branches are not independent channel intermediaries because they are an extension of a manufacturers' organization (Stern et al. 1996). When products are technically complex, as might frequently be the case with products distributed to high-tech customers, this wholesale alternative may be preferred because it eliminates interorganizational power imbalances and the resulting conflicts over distribution policies (Gaski 1984; Frazier and Rody 1991). By eliminating these conflicts, this alternative provides the most control over wholesale distribution strategy.

The third type of wholesaler, agent wholesalers, do not take title to the products they sell and frequently do not hold inventory (Stern et al. 1996). The service provided by agent wholesalers is primarily sales contact because agents function as an alternative to a manufacturer's own sales force. Because compensation for agent wholesalers is generally in commissions on actual sales—tying selling costs directly to sales—agents can provide a lower-cost alternative to manufacturers' sales offices and branches (Rosenbloom 1995). However, agent wholesalers' commissions on sales may present problems for manufacturers targeting high-tech customers. If a manufacturer is selling relatively complex products, these products may require (and the sophisticated high-tech customer may demand) a high level of nonselling tasks, such as product demonstrations, explanations, and after-sales support services. Because agents are not directly compensated for these nonselling tasks, the tasks may not be performed adequately, causing lost initial or repeat sales.

Retailing

A retail transaction is a sale to customers for their personal or household use. Retail transactions include those that occur in retail store and non-store settings (e.g., interactive computer retailing).

Occupying the position nearest the end-use customer in the distribution channel, retailers have a unique understanding of customer demand and product sales patterns (Levy and Weitz 1995; Stern et al. 1996). Because of this position, retailers play an important role. The perceptions relatively sophisticated customers have of a retailer can be an important factor in their decision to purchase products that are somewhat risky because they are frequently new and technologically complex.

Firms marketing products to high-tech customers should be aware of two important issues. The first is the emergence and dominance of "category killers" as a retail format. The second is the role of non-store retailing, particularly the potential offered by multimedia, interactive, and satellite technologies. "Category killers" are retailers characterized by deep merchandise assortments; high sales volumes and merchandise profitability; the use of sophisticated information and distribution systems; customer perceptions of value pricing; and moderate to high levels of customer service. Category killers belong to an emerging group of retailers whose ability to monitor customer trends makes them more likely to take risks, for example, by stocking new merchandise.

The information and distribution systems employed by these retailers enable them to monitor customer preferences and demand patterns with a high level of accuracy. These information and distribution systems, coupled with their customer-service philosophies, further create a high level of product availability. Because of these characteristics, category killers enjoy a high level of customer preference and loyalty (Levy and Weitz 1995; Miller 1995b; Rosenbloom 1995; Stern et al. 1996).

Several of these category killers specialize in products that are frequently sought by high-tech customers (e.g., the consumer electronics offerings at Circuit City). The willingness of these retailers to carry new products they believe will be demanded by their customers makes them a potent force in retailing, and one that offers significant opportunities to the manufacturers of such products.

Although the vast majority of retail sales occurs in stores, the area that is experiencing the largest sales growth is non-store retailing. The non-store retailing formats that have the most potential importance to firms are those formats that use multimedia, interactive, and satellite technologies. These technologies are not limited to the distribution of tangible products; they also offer a substantial potential for distributing consumer service products, such as banking services, and customer support services for computer hardware and software. Access to the Internet is growing rapidly, with most firms establishing commercial pages on the World Wide Web. The potential for interactive distribution of products and services through multimedia, that is, a combination of cable television, telephone, and computers, continues to develop (Stern et al. 1996; Sherman 1994). Distribution, either direct (i.e., to end users) or indirect (through intermediaries, such as wholesalers or retailers), of products (e.g., software) by satellite is another example of a distribution channel that must be considered when targeting high-tech customers.

There are important security considerations that must be addressed regarding these alternative distribution channels and outlets; nevertheless, potentially important market segments are eager to utilize them (Rosenbloom 1995). As an earlier section pointed out (see the discussion of *actualizers* and *strivers*, under Environmental Factors Impacting Distribution to High-Tech Customers), people likely to be targeted by firms marketing to high-tech customer segments tend to be image-conscious, have diverse interests, and be open to new ideas and change. These traits increase the likelihood that such customers want to use retail formats and alternative distribution channels employing new technology and offering alternative, and perhaps more efficient and effective, modes of finding product information and purchasing products and services. Because of the eagerness of these customer segments to access alternative distribution channels, firms marketing to them must pay particular attention to the potential offered by these developing channels.

CONCLUSION

The current pace of technological change means that firms targeting customers who are attracted to, or who demand, products that feature technological innovations stand to reap substantial sales growth. However, this sales growth depends on achieving distribution goals. Firms marketing products that prompt them to identify and target high-tech-customer segments must be aware of the potential for their distribution strategy to significantly affect their ability to attain sales, profitability, and customer satisfaction goals. If distribution decisions fail to assure that these high-tech-customer segments have access to the firm's products, the firm's other efforts toward product development and promotion will be wasted.

This chapter discussed the concepts of specialization and division of labor, and contractual efficiency as the theoretical basis for the importance of marketing channels to a firm's distribution objectives. The impact of sociocultural and technological environmental issues on a firm's distribution strategy was addressed, along with the importance of distribution-intensity considerations. Finally, wholesaling and retailing were examined, including the role of alternative distribution channels arising from the developments in multimedia, interactive, and satellite technologies.

9

Conclusion:
Marketing Strategy Implications

Allan C. Reddy

This chapter presents marketing strategy implications for high-tech product marketers and looks at some important trends.

THE IMPORTANCE OF MARKETING STRATEGY AND PLANNING

We cannot underestimate the importance of strategy and planning in the fast-moving, dynamic business world of today. Generally strategies are directions that organizations take in formulating future plans, policies, procedures, tactics, and actions. Unlike the old-fashioned, long-range planning, strategic planning takes into consideration environmental factors. These factors include such uncontrollable elements as competition, economy, technology, society, consumers, and legal and ethical dimensions. Some of these change more than others. For example, today technological changes are in the forefront affecting every aspect of business. Therefore, to reduce business failure risks, marketers need to be extra diligent in developing their strategic marketing plans and making the plans work.

The marketing-oriented organization understands buyers' needs and wants; it effectively combines and directs the skills and resources of the *entire* organization to provide high levels of satisfaction to its customers. The model of competing, which links R&D, technology, innovation, production, and finance—integrated through marketing's drive to own a market—is the approach that all competitors will take to succeed.

By the mid-1970s some firms—particularly diversified manufacturing companies in such dynamic industries as electronics—recognized that an annual, formal, strategic planning cycle was no longer adequate to respond in a timely manner to rapid changes happening in their global environments. Therefore, they developed the strategic management system to supplement the formal planning cycle. It focuses on the procedures and structures designed to enable organizations to be more responsive to fast-developing opportunities and threats. Some refer to this kind of planning as real-time strategic decision making.

As the twenty-first century unfolds, the need for high-tech marketing grows because most of today's products and services are high-tech or have modern technology integrated into them. In what ways do high-tech marketers differ from regular marketers? What strategies and tactics do they need to succeed in a competitive world filled with constant innovation and shorter product life cycles?

This book touches upon what is deemed to be important up to this point. First, there is no consensus yet on the profile of a high-tech consumer. Some feel that a high-tech consumer draws a relatively high income; is mature, modern in thinking, and innovative; and quick to adopt new products and services. Thus, broadly speaking, in any market—industrial, service, consumer, government, and institutional—there will be a certain portion of that market that comprises high-tech customers; another medium-tech or traditional buyers; and some low-tech (similar to laggards in product adoption curves) customers. Nevertheless, that we can segment markets in this way is a challenging task for marketers. It holds opportunities and threats, however. Innovative organizations see it as an opportunity to tackle the challenges head-on while non-innovative firms stagnate. Business marketers cannot neglect technology life cycles. Firms that ignore changes in technology and continue using old-fashioned methods will confront challenges they cannot manage.

High-tech education is here to stay. Distance-learning alternatives, the Internet, and e-mail are technologies that simply did not exist two decades ago. Educational institutions that are aggressive in using modern technologies continue to prevail and succeed in an age where admitting and retaining students is essential for the existence of most educational institutions.

The Telecommunications Act has many important legal, ethical, and strategy implications for high-tech firms. While the act expands the horizons for businesses, it also restrains businesses in certain aspects.

The high-tech innovators are the essence of high-tech marketing. How can we determine if an individual or organization is an innovator? What measuring scales can we use to identify this characteristic?

High-tech products cannot survive without quality. Without built-in quality, consumers will hesitate to buy products that have no brand name. Consider the success of Netscape, which came up with a high-quality net browser and succeeded in capturing the lion's share of the market. Now, Microsoft's Internet Explorer is trying to capture Netscape's market by improving its quality and making its browser free to users.

Satellites bring high tech to remote corners of the world. People in Bangladesh can see on TV what is happening in the United States and elsewhere live through CNN and other broadcasting services. China is using high tech to educate its masses. India is using satellites to communicate population-control ideas to its people. Consumers are exposed to global brands like Coke, Toyota, IBM, and so on. Of course, consumers in developing countries may not have the purchasing power of those in developed countries. Nevertheless, global corporations cannot ignore high-tech consumers living throughout the world.

Distributing to high-tech markets is a challenge. Traditional channels may not always work. Therefore, innovation occurs in channels of distribution. Outlet malls, the Internet shopping malls, home shopping networks, and direct mail are innovative ways of distributing products and services today.

One can conduct marketing research without ever going to a library. One can find the demographics, shifts in trends, and so forth through a desktop or laptop computer using the Internet.

Finally, marketers cannot expect to be responsible for large inventories anymore because of product changes and shorter product life cycles. Therefore, just-in-time marketing and just-in-time retailing constantly monitor markets; they make and deliver just enough goods so that companies do not suffer losses because of unsold inventories.

In the following paragraphs, issues dealing with high-tech marketing are presented using the traditional four P format.

Product

In both products and services, high tech has caused enormous changes. Product life cycles are getting shorter and shorter, and this creates problems for everyone. Marketers can no longer suggest to manufacturers that they reduce production costs by implementing batch manufacturing, scale economies, and experience-curve concepts that require repetitive production methods. With constant changes in the marketplace, producers cannot take the risk of ending up with large inventories that cannot be sold. Thus, the trend is toward flexible manufacturing. This allows for the manufacturing of new products quickly, compared to traditional methods of batch manufacturing. Levi Strauss and other businesses that deal in the fashion industry have begun to use flexible manufacturing successfully.

In televisions, the trend is to manufacture and market high-definition TVs—big televisions with screens up to 60 inches in rear projection sets, and up to 40 inches in tube sets. Thirty-five-inch sets are becoming popular now, replacing the 32- and 27-inch sets.

In transportation, airlines that are fuel-efficient and economical, without compromising comfort quality, are popular. Airbus Industries from Europe, with its Airbus series, is a tough competitor for Boeing in manufacturing and marketing passenger and cargo aircraft. In many parts of the world, Boeing aircrafts are replaced with Airbus planes because of their low initial cost as well as low operating costs.

In computers and electronics, changes are happening at an astonishing rate.

Not too long ago the 486 chip was popular in computers. Now, the pentium chip at 200 megahertz can do most jobs at lightning speeds. Modern desktop computers have 16MB or more of RAM memory and disk capacity exceeding 1GB. With Windows 95, multi-tasking is possible. One can work on a word processor and a spreadsheet, and perform a web search simultaneously. In the music industry, digital music is becoming a standard. In health care, laser surgeries are gaining popularity. In communication, cellular phones are increasing in sales. The following paragraph suggests one important high-tech innovation in each field mentioned:

1. Television—HDTV, 35–40", 60" sets in rear projection, surround sound, picture-in-picture, DSS, flat screens, Internet TVs.
2. Education—Computers, distance learning, e-mail, the Internet, cyber-universities.
3. Transportation—High-speed trains, fuel-efficient aircraft that can travel long distances with more passenger comforts.
4. Food and nutrition—High tech in food manufacturing, packaging, and delivery. Better vitamins.
5. Health care—Laser surgeries, heart transplants, artificial limbs, cloning.
6. Exercise and fitness—Athletic shoes, fitness equipment.
7. Computers—size, memory, storage, operation (CD), software, artificial intelligence.
8. Communication—Cellular phones.
9. Supermarkets—Super K, Super Wal-Mart.
10. Shopping Malls—Internet shopping malls.
11. Publishing—Electronic publishing.
12. Classroom lectures—Computers in classrooms.

Promotion

Promoting high-tech products is challenging. Most of them are expensive as manufacturers skim the cream of the market to recover costs of research and development as fast as they can. High prices are no longer a barrier to marketing high-tech products because of the increase in two-income families. But consumers will not venture buying a new product if it is not properly promoted. This requires a great deal of planning and execution involving advertising, public relations, and so on. The legal and ethical aspects of promotion also need to be considered.

Pricing

Most high-tech products tend to be expensive mainly because manufacturers try to recover initial costs for research and development as quickly as possible. But the trick is making people buy the product. Netscape gave away their browsers free to attract customers. It proved successful; now, Microsoft and others are trying the same technique.

Distribution

The Internet is a new method of distribution allowing consumers to buy software through directly downloading.

Marketing Management Strategies

Summing up, to deal with the twenty-first century's high-tech consumer, marketing management must be prepared to deal with the dynamics of planning and conduct aggressive promotion of high-quality products. High-tech products cannot be taken for granted; organizations need to continuously train workers, to keep up with the fast pace.

Appendix A: Researching Industry Information Electronically

Ruth Pagell

This chapter reveals the techniques one can use to quickly gather information about a particular industry through electronic research. Similar methods can be used to obtain information on any subject electronically. This is a boon for organizations marketing to high-tech consumers and for high-tech consumers seeking facts about products, as well as general information through the Internet.

In today's global marketplace, researching an industry requires not only learning about the industry itself but also finding out about different countries and their companies. Effective business intelligence requires analyzing the industry, the companies within the industry, and the countries in which they operate. As an example of the breadth of electronic information available, we will look at readily accessible material on the Asian computer industry. Most of the material concerns the Japanese computer industry and its competition with both the United States and Europe. However, information is available for the rest of Asia. The consensus from the last six months points to a continued growth of the computer industry in most of Asia, with continued problems within the Japanese computer industry.

INFORMATION SOURCES

We can divide the information sources in two ways: the intelligence features they cover and their electronic format.

INTELLIGENCE FEATURES: We rely on three major types of information: the market (the countries and their demographics), the industry, and the companies.

This chapter was originally published in *Access from Singapore*, September 1994. Reprinted with the permission of the author.

ELECTRONIC FORMATS: We use three major electronic access methods: CD-ROMs, online files, and the Internet.

In earlier articles (Access #4/5 and #6/7), we examined CD-ROMs and online files with ASEAN business information. The sources that we listed in those articles can be used for researching the Asian computer industry. Especially useful products are

Database	CD-ROM Provider(s)	Online File/ Source
TEXT		
Predicasts F&S + Text Specific product information	SilverPlatter, IAC	PROMT
ABI/Inform (Global) General overview of industry coverage	UMI	ABI/INFORM
COIN (Reuters) Local reports from Reuters	SilverPlatter	COMLINE
COMLINE Japanese perspective; technical	SilverPlatter	COMLINE
COUNTRY AND INDUSTRY DATA		
National Trade Data Bank Market reports, U.S. trade data	U.S. Dept. of Commerce	NTDB[1] on L/N[2]
U.S. Industrial Outlook	U.S. International Trade Administration on NTDB	Internet
RELATED INFORMATION (online and on disk)		
Corporate Affiliations (Dialog File 513) Major companies and their parents/subsidiaries		
World Companies Directory (Gale Research CD-ROM) Smaller companies interested in trade		
Kompass Asia-Pacific (CD-ROM and Dialog File 518) Product-specific listings		
D&B Market Identifies Asia-Pacific (Dialog File 518) Country-specific company listings		
ELECTRONIC SOURCES OF COUNTRY INFORMATION		
EIU Country Reports and Profiles Economic and political		L/N, DIALOG, CD-ROM
Walden Reports Economic with business applications		L/N
Overseas Business Reports U.S. perspective, with trade focus		L/N, NTDB

| *Market Reports* | L/N, NTDB |
| U.S. perspective, with trade focus | |

| *CIA World Fact Book* | Internet |
| Economic Data | |

Notes:

1. NTDB is no longer published. It has been replaced by *U.S. Global Trade Outlook*.
2. L/N = LEXIS/NEXIS.

The commercial online systems have a variety of databases which include industry, product, and country information. You will find local newspapers, country reports, computer newsletters, and directory databases of Asian companies.

CASE STUDY: COMPUTER INDUSTRY IN ASIA

One of the best and most expensive commercial sources for current articles about Asia is in the LEXIS/NEXIS World, Regional, and Country libraries. An example is the China Library. By using the specific library, each search statement costs less, and the search results should be more relevant. Economist Intelligence Unit (EIU) Country Reports and Country Pofiles for more than 150 countries have for years been the main academic source of comparable country economic and political analyses (see Figure A.1). Use the EIU annual Country Profiles and quarterly reports, and companion newsletters *Business Asia* and *Business China* for authoritative data and analyses. Two other EIU publications, *Investing, Licensing and Trading in . . .* and *Financing Foreign Operations*, provide a high-end, quality information package. These very specialized publications are expensive in print form. They may be used occasionally online on either LEXIS/NEXIS or Dialog File 627. EIU offers two CD-ROM versions. One, through Dialog Ondisc, is arranged by region. The other, provided by SilverPlatter, is by publication.

Of a more practical nature is *Financing Foreign Operations*. Topics included in this publication for January 1, 1994 (from LEXIS/NEXIS):

1. Countertrade
2. Withholding
3. Business overview
4. Economic environment
5. Corporate financial strategies
6. Currency outlook
7. Currency behavior and forecast.

Another useful EIU report is *Investing, Licensing and Trading Abroad*, with important information for doing business in Asian countries. *Walden Reports*,

Figure A.1
Extract of EIU Country Report from LEXIS/NEXIS (Country Profile, November 1, 1993)

```
HEADLINE: Employment:   Labor force by sector  (m; year-end)
```

	1986	1987	1988	1989	1990	1991
State-owned units of which: industry, government	93.3	96.5	99.8	101.1	103.5	106.6
agencies & people's organiza-	39.6	40.9	42.3	42.7	43.6	44.7
tions	7.4	7.8	8.2	8.6	9.0	9.5
Self-employed in towns of which: commerce, catering &	4.8	5.7	6.6	6.5	6.7	7.6
other services	3.4	3.9	4.4	4.4	4.3	4.9
Total incl others	512.8	527.8	543.3	553.3	567.4	583.6

Source: State Statistical Bureau, *China Statistical Yearbook.* Copyright 1993 Economic Intelligence Unit.

provided by *Financial Times*, are targeted specifically for the business user with information about culture, infrastructure, and trade. Subheadings in a *Walden* report may include:

Ethnic Makeup

Banking and Business Hours

Local Customs

Top Banks and Insurance Companies

Basic Regulatory Structure

Stock Exchanges

Trading Regulation

Industry and Production

Transportation

Communications and Newspapers

Figure A.2
Extract of China's External Debt from DIALOG ($ million)

	1985	1990	1991	1992	1993	1994	1995
Total foreign indebtedness	16,722	52,554	60,851	69,321	80,625	93,150	102,750
Public medium & long term	9,963	45,319	50,551	58,475	68,125	77,625	85,625
Commercial creditors	11,658	37,584	43,761	50,219	60,755	73,000	82,600
Percent of total debt	71.7	72.4	71.9	72.4	75.4	78.4	80.4

File 627.
Source: Country Risk Service, March 1, 1994

Country Risk Report: China

Other reports look at country risk. Sometimes, the size of the potential market, as with China, may outweigh the risks. The March 1994 EIU *Country Risk Service* (formerly *Economic Risk Service*) gives China an overall rating of *B* with a political and policy risk of *C*. It also lists the country's external debt, predicting an increase in total foreign indebtedness of over 500 percent between 1985 and 1995 (see Figure A.2).

Industry Intelligence

Online systems include "off-the-shelf" market research reports from major market research houses. These reports also are expensive in print form and may be equally as expensive online, but cost can be contained in electronic format by printing only those pages that have the information you want.

While there are several reports on the computer industry worldwide, only the Japanese companies, such as Fujitsu and NEC, along with U.S. and European market leaders for hardware, software, and service are discussed (see Table A.1). Fujitsu, which has strengthened its market share by the acquisition of United Kingdom's ICL, is listed as the second largest supplier in the world while NEC is listed as third. Fujitsu and NEC rank second and fourth as hardware and software manufacturers as well.

Fujitsu is listed as the fourth largest minicomputer producer with 11.2 percent market share; NEC is right behind with 9.3 percent. Positions are reversed for personal computers, with NEC listed as fourth and Fujitsu fifth. Fujitsu is also listed as the fourth largest producer of workstations.

Table A.1
The World's Largest Hardware Manufacturers by Revenue (Top Five in Each Category), 1993

	Revenues ($m)	% Share of World Market
Mainframe		
IBM	8,190	29.1
Fujitsu	4,431	15.7
Hitachi	4,044	14.4
NEC	3,079	11.0
Unisys	1,966	7.0
Others	6,434	22.9
Total	8,144	100.0

Another report deals with the magnetic and opto-magnetic storage, the computer storage market, and current worldwide market shares.

The report notes that the worldwide picture hasn't changed significantly in the last five years and is not expected to change much in the next five years. The United States has the most manufacturing capability, followed by Japan and Europe. The report further discloses that although some manufacturing and assembly are performed in countries such as Singapore, these are performed for U.S. or Japanese companies.

Market Reports (LEXIS/NEXIS or National Trade Data Bank—NTDB)

There are presently over 15,000 market reports available on the NTDB. However, there is no uniform reporting by country and industry. You may or may not find what you need. For example, reports exist for the Chinese automotive industry, but not the Chinese computer industry. The October 1993 *Country Marketing Plan* has a section on computers and peripherals. It recommends that the most promising sectors are operating system services, database management services, and network services.

Much of the current business information on China appears in news articles. The information is timely, but not authoritative. The Xinhua General Overseas News Service reported on April 19, 1994, that China's largest computer enterprise has devised a market plan to compete with the major worldwide companies, such as IBM and Compaq, who have entered the Chinese market. The corporation sold more than 27,000 microcomputers, or 7 percent of the Chinese market, to rank top among the country's computer enterprises and companies. "Almost all of the world's well-known computer manufacturers and companies are betting on the Chinese market, the potentially largest single market of the world."

Official Chinese statistics show that the market share for Chinese-made computers has declined. The news service also wrote in March 1994 that computer sales expected to rise 30 percent that year.

Newsletters

COMLINE database, in either DATASTAR or LEXIS/NEXIS, has a special report on computers—COMLINE Daily News Computers. A February 15, 1994, article stated that NEC's share was estimated to be 49.0 percent of the Japanese market, down 2.8 points, with Apple second; IBM third; and Fujitsu fourth.

Companies in the Computer Industry

The industry is made up of companies located in the Asian region and multinational companies conducting business in Asia. Lists are available in the directory electronic databases, such as Kompass Asia-Pacific and Dun and Bradstreet Asia-Pacific. The latter includes a much wider range of countries.

Extel Cards, a database of public companies and news stories about them (on DIALOG, DATASTAR, LEXIS/NEXIS, FT Profile, and CD-ROM), may be used to identify new international deals. It reported in November 1993 that Informatics Holdings Ltd., a Singaporian company, has set up its first computer education and training center in China—Informatics College. The company has incorporated a new subsidiary in Hong Kong, Informatics Education (People's Republic of China).

Identifying the Largest Companies

D&B Asia-Pacific Market Identification Report Dialog File 518 can be used to generate a list of the largest companies within a country. An example for Taiwan is listed in Figure A.3.

Kompass Asia-Pacific can be used to identify computer companies based on very specific product lines, but there is no ranking capability. The database, which had 373 computer companies in Hong Kong, 2,166 in Singapore, and 2,192 in Teikoku, includes almost 200,000 Japanese companies on Western systems DIALOG and DATASTAR, and includes rankings within industries. The entire file of over 900,000 companies is available in Japan.

New Company Information Source

The Dallas, Texas, firm, AsiaInfo, is a new provider of electronic Chinese

Figure A.3
Largest Computer Companies in Taiwan

Company Name	Country Name	Sales Local $	Sales US $
ACER INCORPORATED	TAIWAN	11,923,246,000	450,954,841
TAIWAN INTERNATIONAL STANDARD	TAIWAN	7,127,739,000	269,581,657
ELITE-GROUP COMPUTER SYSTEMS C	TAIWAN	7,060,350,000	267,032,905
MITAC INTERNATIONAL CORP	TAIWAN	6,469,426,000	244,683,283
DELTA ELECTRONIC INC	TAIWAN	6,426,479,000	243,058,964
FIRST INTERNATIONAL COMPUTER I	TAIWAN	5,115,084,000	193,460,061
INVENTA ELECTRONICS CO LTD	TAIWAN	4,647,113,000	175,760,703
CAL-COMP ELECTRONICS INC	TAIWAN	4,582,763,296	173,326,902
CHUNTEX ELECTRONICS CO LTD	TAIWAN	4,230,777,000	160,014,259
CHICONY ELECTRONICS CO LTD	TAIWAN	4,186,841,487	158,352,552
COMPAL ELECTRONICS INC	TAIWAN	4,091,234,000	154,736,536
COPAM ELECTRONICS CORPORATION	TAIWAN	4,080,600,000	154,334,342
TWINHEAD INTERNATIONAL CORP	TAIWAN	4,034,635,000	152,595,877
TWINHEAD INTERNATIONAL CORP	TAIWAN	3,823,468,000	144,609,228
DATAEXPERT CORP	TAIWAN	3,800,000,000	143,721,634

information. It is a joint venture between BDI Group, Inc. in Dallas and Wanfang Data, Inc. in Beijing, China.

The business-related database, China's Enterprises and Companies Database (CECDB), covers all types of commercial, industrial, and service establishments. It is available online, on diskette, and on CD-ROM. You may search by U.S. Standard Industrial Classification codes, type of business, product, province, city, post code, sales figures, number of employees, and import/export indicator codes. The AsiaInfo database includes over 100,000 public and private companies in China. This represents over 90 percent coverage of China's medium- to large-sized companies (a sample company profile is shown in Figure A.4).

Some of the major industry groupings are apparel, petrochemicals and coal products, construction materials, fabricated metal products, and import and export firms. There are over 2,000 computer and electronics companies. The company database is supplemented by an online "Daily" and a "HotLine News"

Figure A.4
China Company and Incorporation Profile

```
NAME  :          CHINA PETROCHEMICAL CORPORATION,
                 QILU PETROCHEMICAL CORPORATION
         ABB.:   QLPCC
PRESIDENT :      Li Chengyou
 PROVINCE :      Shandong
     CITY :      Zibo
  ADDRESS :      Linzi, Zibo, Shandong, China
    PHONE :      (0533)710762
    CABLE:       0172
      FAX :      (0533) 710940
POST CODE :      255436
EMPLOYEES :      48500
 ENGINEERS:      1100
OUTPUT VALUE:    582000 ( Thousand USD )
     SALE :      613300 ( Thousand USD )
FOREIGN EARNINGS:  31000 ( Ten thousand USD )
ORGANIZATION CODE:   E
  PRODUCT :
 BUSINESS :      Gasoline, Kerosene, Diesel Oil, Naphtha,
Coke...
KEY WORDS:       Gasoline; Kerosene; Diesel Oil; Sulfur;
Asphalt;...

SIC CODE :       2911, 5172, 2819

SAMPLE RECORD: China's Enterprises & Companies Database
(CECDB0)
```

with a direct electronic feed directly from China. Daily stock reports and weekly investment opportunities are promised.

Using the Internet

Researchers want their information free. While the Internet is not free to the organizations providing the access, it is often free to the individual user.

A businessperson considering the Internet as a means to access information about a corporate intelligence topic, such as the computer industry in Asia, must realize the limitations of this service. Most traditional print and electronic sources of business information are *not* available free on the Internet. Furthermore, neither the information sources nor the type of searching necessary to pull together complex subjects to find relevant articles yet exist. Commercial services, such as DIALOG and LEXIS/NEXIS, may be accessed through the Internet, to avoid telecommunications connections. Keeping these limitations in mind, researchers with access to the Internet but who do not have access to commercial sources might try locating the following source.

Figure A.5
Internet Record of the CIA World Fact Book

```
China, Header
  Affiliation:
     (also see separate Taiwan entry)

  Geography
     International disputes
     Natural resources
     Environment:
  People
  Government
  Economy
      National product:    GNP $NA
      Inflation rate (consumer prices) 5.4% (1992)
      Unemployment rate: 2.3% in urban areas (1992)
      Industries:
      Exchange rates: yuan (Y) per US$1 - 5.7640 (January
      1993),
      5.5146 (1992), 5.3234 (1991),4.7832 (1990), 3.7651
      (1989),
      3.7221 (1988)
  Communications [includes transportation]
  Defense Forces
[From: Project Gutenberg  P. O. Box  2782  Champaign, IL
61825]
```

Note: NTDB is availiable on the Internet as part of STAT-USA for $150 a year.
Source: World Fact Book 1993 of the CIA (split into countries) from the Gutenberg Project.

For background information on a country, including an overview of the major country intelligence indicators, population, geography, infrastructure, income, and industry sectors, locate one of the many Internet sites that have loaded the CIA World Fact Book. Unlike the expensive commercial sources, this source is free and not copyrighted. However, the information it includes is less specific to business applications. The outline of the report below was accessed by performing a ''VERONICA'' search on CIA World and identifying the site with the most recent edition, 1993. An outline of a sample report appears in Figure A.5.

CONCLUSION

Using a variety of online and ondisc products supplemented by web sites, you can locate a wide range of material on the Asian computer industry. The information, however, is still fragmented and expensive. In volatile markets, such as China, using online is still preferable to CD-ROMs and web searches, when current, thorough, and reliable information is needed. A similar strategy can be used to locate Asian information in other industries.

Appendix B: Internet Marketing

Allan C. Reddy

This chapter introduces the history, background, and salient aspects of Internet marketing. The Internet is no longer the techno fad of a decade ago, a cyber-heaven of computer nerds and research scientists (Miller 1995a). It is now increasingly popular among businesses as an avenue for marketing their products and services. The system is growing so rapidly that commercial users on the Internet are expected to reach 50 million by the year 2000. Many people, however, still see the Internet as a noncommercial academic and technical environment (Buckley 1995).

The commercial Internet is the fastest-growing part of cyberspace. An Internet address on a business card is the latest craze. The Internet is not owned by any single company or nation. The only real restriction placed upon users is by the virtual community itself (Solomon 1994).

DOING BUSINESS ON THE INTERNET

Doing business on the Internet will become a regular activity. It offers a low-cost delivery system with color graphics, audio, and video clips. It is accessible from diverse locations, available 24 hours daily, 365 days a year. While advertisers and marketers on the Internet reap profits, consumers can benefit from buying their products. It is faster, and online support forums provide advice that is not found in manuals, catalogs, or brochures. To succeed on the Internet, innovation is the key. Therefore, new ideas and new ways of marketing products and services are making their debut on the Internet regularly.

The World Wide Web also serves as an efficient distribution channel. It offers to certain classes of providers participation in a market in which distribution costs or the cost of sales decline to zero. Businesses on the web transfer more of the selling function to the customer through online ordering and the use of fill-out forms that bring the transactions to a speedy completion. Industrial marketers find reduced errors, reduced time and overhead costs in information processing, and reduced costs to suppliers by electronically finding online databases of bid opportunities, online abilities to submit bids, and online reviews of awards.

Businesses can communicate effectively with e-mail; call attention to new products; link to distant branch offices; and provide cost-effective, high-quality customer support through bulletin boards, discussion groups, message boards, and the Frequently Asked Questions (FAQ) pages. E-mail systems help businesses avoid telephone tag; they further allow firms to send large bytes of information quickly and inexpensively to anywhere in the world. By using the Internet to hold discussion groups, technical departments can receive answers to significant questions from experts worldwide.

With the Internet, firms can increase their competitive advantage, prepare presentations, conduct research, learn more about the competition, and get to the marketplace first with a new product or service through product announcements. The companies that are establishing an Internet presence now will be ahead of the game (Miller 1995a). As advanced communications continue to expand across the globe, the Internet will become increasingly important for business organizations and their ability to plug into consumers. Is there any other marketing medium that a consumer can reach 24 hours a day from all over the world?

Companies are also using the Internet to take advantage of outsourcing services—firms that do certain tasks, such as payroll. Voice, images, music, and video are converging on a digital substate. The information superhighway is prompting innovation in many companies. For example, right now consumers can receive a channel on cable that will allow them to select and play Sega games over the cable line.

The technology that will be inspired by the Internet will give new life to cable and telephone companies. Soon, Georgia Power will offer the consumer interactive cable capabilities and telephone services.

Companies can now prevent credit-card fraud with the technology developed for the Internet. This technology prevents thieves from withdrawing on a person's account, by giving the customer a password or an identification number. Students can access information services to aid them in their research and homework, and they can interact with others. Teachers feel that these services give the students a chance to learn and to feel more at ease with their surroundings and classmates. The Internet also allows people to play life-like games when they are thousands of miles away. Consumers can gather information and send it just as businesses can, and soon they will be able to view 500 channels.

The Internet is also a source of many electronic games that both elders and kids love to play. One can get new games faster through here than through the marketplace, by downloading the games directly from the firms' home pages.

Disadvantages

Undoubtedly, the advantages far outweigh the disadvantages. Accumulated industry experience and quantitative evidence strongly suggest that the primary barrier to consumer adoption of the web as a commercial medium is the ease of access. The secondary barriers are ease of use, price, and risk, including such factors as privacy and security. Also, customers may not have access to the Internet in sufficient numbers. Therefore, businesses may need to maintain two information systems.

Security in transactions is still uncertain, although some web browsers claim encryption is supposed to provide enough security to make credit-card transactions over the Internet safe. Also, Internet ethics, or "netiquette," is still an evolving field. In news groups of Usenet, one often finds "flaming" and use of profanity. Flaming is verbally criticizing and abusing others. People need to be educated about these, and etiquette must be observed in Internet communications. Copyright laws are difficult to enforce because anything that is available on the Internet is publicly accessible; therefore, there is less control over its use and distribution.

The Internet and Direct Marketing

Is the Internet a new form of direct marketing? The traditional method for marketing is to approach prequalified markets based on demographic and psychographic characteristics. If an Internet user "hits" an advertiser's web site, it is more likely that he or she is interested in the articles, products, or services that the advertiser has to offer. Today almost all of the Fortune 500 companies have launched marketing programs on the World Wide Web. Such companies as General Electric, IBM, Rockwell, and others have jumped on the web to promote their products and to get their message to new customers (Janah 1995). To enhance its image to customers and prospects throughout the world, IBM is using the power of the web to announce new products and to provide corporate information. Many firms announce job opportunities as well.

Magazine Subscriptions

Several magazines have attempted making the transition to the new electronic medium, and they are finding that integration with customers and advertisers can be tricky. Magazines are now understanding how to turn early-learning experiences into revenue-generating products. The Internet is attempting to expose people to novel things and give them something in new media that they cannot get in traditional print (Kelly 1995). Customers do not have to wait for issues to arrive in the mail or until they hit the newsstands. All customers need do is turn on their computer, and the latest publications are at their fingertips.

Environmentalists like this idea because less paper is used; therefore, publishers are saving trees. A consequence of this advancement may be an increase in cost for the user or subscriber.

The Internet is nonproprietary; therefore, users pay no fee. However, services like CompuServe, Prodigy, America Online, and Microsoft Network charge their users tolls that range between 5 percent and 20 percent for sales from specific vendors. When year 2000 rolls around and there could be more than a hundred million consumers on the Internet, we may see ad agencies and advertising-supported magazines go under as businesses learn to communicate directly to consumers in cyberspace (Kelly 1995). The most effective promotional tool has been the ability of the web to carry the message of marketing and communication professionals to target groups. Here, such promotional information as new product announcements, product catalogs, and seminar training schedules can be put on the web.

Mail-Order Catalogs

The explosion in electronic marketing is the beginning of a new-age communication that provides marketing executives with some powerful tools to reach their audience. The most exciting aspect is that it provides two of the most important aspects of modern marketing philosophies—the ability to target select groups of buyers and to continue interactive dialogue. This traditional technique of reaching audiences is quickly noticing new competition—not in print but on the computer screen.

Most companies just want to know how best to sell their goods and services online. By using the Internet, companies do not incur the costs of printing and mailing catalogs; furthermore, they can be updated within minutes. These advantages not only allow small companies an unprecedented opportunity to expand but also to offer precise and speedy service to their customers.

Electronic marketing on the World Wide Web (WWW) develops an affinity between the customer and seller through a closer and more intimate relationship. Here customers can get information on demand that relates precisely to their exact needs and develops a strong feeling of being highly served by the selling company (Zbar 1995).

Because customers and prospects alike want to feel a personal relationship with the companies providing their needs, the idea of getting personal information and communicating interactively through e-mail or other electronic means dramatically enhances the company's image in the buyer's mind.

Is the Internet a new tool for public relations (PR)? PR has traditionally been a way for advertisers to keep in touch with their public, by sending long-form messages that are educational. Internet PR is exciting because it allows a firm to receive immediate consumer feedback and explore new levels of goodwill. The interactive feature of this global computer network enables a PR firm to enhance a program with short videos and sound clips, making digital public relations a solid partner with traditional media techniques.

Unregulated Medium

Just twelve months ago, the thought of advertising on the Internet was the farthest thing from the minds of marketing executives. And the very idea curled the hair of Internet veterans. For 20 years the old Internet held firm to its conviction that advertising and marketing held no place on the Internet; it was far above such commercial activity. But the WWW and its appeal to marketing professionals has completely changed that (Coppett and Staples 1993). Today it has attracted the attention of Madison Avenue marketing executives, who are creating special groups within large advertising agencies to serve their clients' needs on the Internet.

From Philip Morris and DeKuyper to Coors, major companies are considering advertising their products online. On the Internet there are no rules, so anything goes (Solomon 1994). The dominant question today for tobacco, liquor, and beer advertisers is, Is cyberspace more like television or magazines? These companies must also consider which line of advertising will be the best for their individual products. Spirit marketers, though not beer marketers, have voluntarily abstained from advertising on radio and television since the early days of broadcasting.

Coors Brewing Company is doing some of its best marketing, by printing its Internet address on its Zima bottle labels. This visual strategy to catch younger customers has been quite successful; there are a variety of sound bites and icons that can be used by customers (Taylor 1995). Jim Beam offers a ''virtual bar'' on the Internet, but a user must be 21 or older (Warner 1995). DeKuyper offers drink recipes and a cartoon saloon for its drinkers' enjoyment. The Federal Communications Commission does not have jurisdiction over the Internet or any commercial online service. To date, Congress has not considered regulating online advertising. The telecommunications bill makes no mention of the subject. But the FCC plans a conference on consumer protection on the Internet (Warner 1995).

Unsolicited advertising does indeed take place every day on the Internet; one company even sells access to more than one million Internet addresses for direct advertising. Unsolicited advertising is a grey area of Internet culture and therefore requires very careful planning and execution to avoid the wrath of an extremely vocal community.

Security

An Internet connection brings potential rewards and risks to the organization. Intrusion by outsiders represents a major threat to corporate information, information systems, and business operations. Strong security measures are necessary to repel both the casual and the determined hacker (Cleland 1995). When you are connected to the Internet, by definition, the Internet is connected to you. Although online commerce looks promising, impediments remain. The commercialization of electronic space is proceeding, despite warnings that the information superhighway does not yet have adequate safeguards against piracy. By far the most serious is the security problem posed by dishonest hackers, the masked highwaymen of the information age. Expert hackers attack Internet-connected systems regularly. The sophistication and persistence of attacks have increased steadily (Cleland 1995). Attacks are prompting growing concern for the integrity of corporate networks. Potential intruders are growing in number and expertise, and they increasingly use automated penetration tools to identify and exploit weaknesses in hosts connected to the Internet. Once inside, a hacker can cause problems that range from annoying to catastrophic. Intruders can disrupt business operations, steal, modify or destroy data, take control of computers, and install Trojan horse programs that can hide on the network while performing various functions for the hacker (Bayne 1994).

Marketers are entering the Internet en masse to sell goods and services, and many expect to have transaction addresses. Companies are understandably wary about sending purchase orders over unsecured computer networks, and consumers often hesitate to send their credit-card numbers, too.

Advertising on the Internet

Advertising reach is estimated at more than 30 million worldwide computer users, and this reach is ballooning. More people connect to the Internet each day, either through commercial online services like Prodigy, or with direct connections from Internet-access providers (Buckley 1995). *The Chicago Tribune Magazine* reports that the number of Internet users is increasing by 10 percent each month.

How It Works

The Internet is several computer networks linked together for sending and retrieving data. It is a marvelous tool for receiving information from all over the world. Businesspeople can find data that enable them to develop a competent competitive advantage. Doctors can send and receive patients' charts from anywhere in the world in a matter of seconds. Teachers are using the Internet to give students the opportunity to find more information.

Many people are fascinated by the information superhighway. However, it is just another method used to send and receive information. A study concerning the Internet was commissioned by the Audit Bureau of Circulation. This audit, which consisted of 2,000 American adults, revealed that only half of the participants had heard of the information superhighway, and that most of these participants had only a limited knowledge of the service. Many were unaware of

Internet marketers' role in the transmission of this information. Nevertheless, as technologies change (and they will) the need for computer networks will increase.

The Internet was born 20 years ago, as a U.S. Defense Department network called ARPANET. It was designed as an experimental network for the military to keep the minimum amount of information about its computer clients. To send information over the network, a computer placed the information in a packet called Internet Protocol (IP). After the information was gathered, it was then sent to its proper address. The computers alone were responsible for making sure that the tasks were accomplished. Therefore, it was possible for each computer to communicate with one another. The developers of the Internet, responding to market pressure, began to put their IP software on every conceivable type of computer. This became the only way that computers manufactured by different companies could communicate.

About ten years later, Ethernet Local Area Networks (LAN) and computer workstations made their presence in the market. When the IP was first introduced, it was designed specifically to communicate with the mainframe, in addition to others. The introduction of workstations created a new demand: rather than connecting to a single large time-sharing computer per site, organizations wanted to connect the ARPANET to their entire LAN. This provided the means for LAN-based computers to access an ARPANET facility. Networks became a popular issue in the late 1970s.

During the 1970s the National Science Foundation (NSF) designed one of the most important computer network systems. In the early 1980s NSF developed five super computer centers. At that time the only super computers available were for weapons developers and huge corporations. These centers allowed everyone to access the network. The NSF promoted universal educational access by funding campus connections only if they spread the access around. Many universities are now connected to the Internet, and the NSF is planning to connect secondary and primary schools to continue growth. If the Internet is placed in the school systems, it will most likely prepare students for future uses of the Internet. This will give them the ability and courage to learn how to operate a computer. Right now there are probably 39,000 industrial or educational subscribers. They have estimated that there are around 30 million Internet users, and this figure should double in 1996.

The Internet Society

The Internet has no president or CEO. The authority over the information superhighway rests with the Internet Society, or ISOC. The ISOC is basically a voluntary membership organization that uses Internet technology to encourage global information exchange. It has a group of innovative volunteers called the Internet Architecture Board (IAB), which meets regularly to discuss problems, appropriate resources, and decide standards for the Internet. Different computers have different languages. One of the functions of the IAB is to develop software to match these different languages.

The Internet is basically a huge computer network that allows users to send and receive pictures, text, and voice from any location around the globe. Although the Internet seems very difficult, the steps involved in sending information over the network are quite simple. If a business has access to a network (all that is required are a computer, a modem, and a network subscriber), it may send and receive messages throughout the network. After the information has been entered into the computer, it proceeds through a set of steps:

Step 1—The message is coded, then routed over many independent networks to its final destination. The link to the network may be telephone or cable lines, or radio transmissions. The most common links are fiber optics and satellites.

Step 2—The code is examined by computers as the information travels through the network. The computer reads the code and determines where the information will be sent next.

Step 3—The network has the capability to select the least-crowded route when it sends information to the user. It is common to have a different route when sending the same message to the same computer.

Step 4—The Internet has a main "backbone" in the United States. This backbone has a huge capacity and is maintained by the NSF. As information travels to its destination, it may or may not cross this backbone.

Step 5—The information reaches its destination.

To better illustrate the sequence of steps in sending data, please refer to Figure B.1. Each square represents one or more computer systems. The circles represent computer networks. These networks are linked together by cables (i.e., radio waves, satellite transmission, fiber optics, or communication cables), which send the information to the various computers. In Figure B.1, these cables are represented as thick lines. Moreover, the thick lines show the possible direction the information can travel.

There is no such thing as an Internet company that collects fees from all of the network companies or users (Krol 1995). Every subscriber pays for their part. The NSF pays for its Internet service. Likewise, other institutes pay for their research networks. Network companies get together to decide how they will link themselves with each together and fund their interconnections. Therefore, when the Internet is down, it is more likely that there is a problem with the connection of the network server rather than with the Internet itself. Also, the companies listed on the Internet could be at fault.

The Resources Available

By now most people are familiar with the fact that one can access or send data over the Internet. Nevertheless, there are more resources available which include:

Figure B.1
Illustration of How the Internet Works

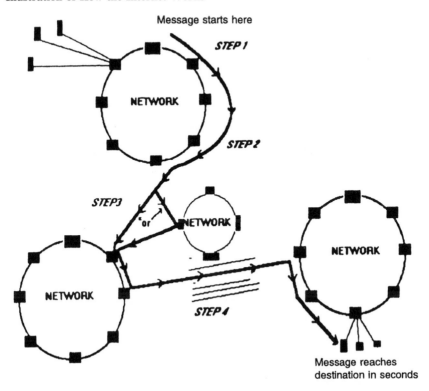

Electronic mail (e-mail)

News

Gopher

Telnet

Archie

FTP

Listservs

The first exposure to the Internet for most people is in the form of e-mail. This is basically a service that allows people to use a computer to send and receive messages to and from different addresses. The network news (News) is used for discussion topics or as a bulletin board to examine social issues, scientific research, and miscellaneous subjects. Gopher allows the user to explore and access the resources on the Internet. This can be achieved through Telnet or FTP, but Gopher takes care of identifying addresses, where the others do not.

Telnet gives the user the capabilities to connect directly to a host computer. This allows the user's computer to act as if it were a terminal directly linked to the system; the user can process all the information on the host computer. Archie is a tool for locating information and access it with File Transfer Protocol (FTP). Listservs are like e-mail but are used more as a bulletin board for discussions.

Undesirable Changes

Many companies will make some undesirable changes before the information superhighway reaches the whole world. For example, the Internet will put people out of work. Banks are going to downsize their staff in certain departments when the real information superhighway is constructed. Some teachers believe that students will depend too much on computers and will spend less time developing the skills needed to communicate with others. Lack of communication skills will be a problem in today's competitive workplace.

Internet Environment

Staffing the Internet will be a major issue in the future. There are already enough technical wizards who can transfer this technology into new businesses. However, the search is on for qualified professionals who can adapt to these new tools in the work environment (Messmer 1996). It is very simple for a technocrat to develop another tool, but to learn how to operate the new tool requires patience and skill for the amateur to become an expert.

Business Environment

In the past, businesses relied on the postal service to deliver important documents. If the company did not want to use the postal service, they would have to rely on their own resources—hand delivery. This method was time-consuming and unreliable. The time lag could allow other businesses to meet the demands of the customer. With today's massive technology, firms can send documents via computer network to their customers within seconds. This enables businesses to deliver information quickly and receive fast results.

Firm can collect and distribute many forms of information. For example, an American magazine company can access a computer in London to get mailing lists. These mailing lists can be adapted to fit a target market in London by accessing marketing information from another computer in England. A database can be formed in a matter of hours—in the past it took much time and energy. The database can be processed into a computer that mails the magazines to that target market. It helps companies select new markets, thus formulating their marketing functional strategies. The Internet is also used to aid corporations examining their competition and customer needs.

Information is also readily available for customer use. It can aid a customer in selecting the right product (e.g., buying a car) without going to a seller. Customers may even find information on the product (e.g., in online consumer reports) to help them in making a better purchase. A person can contact magazine companies, car dealerships, or any company that has advertised on the Internet, to receive information on the product or service and even place an order.

Businesses are now shifting from manufacturing to service industries. A Washington think tank believes that the Internet could create more than $320 billion annually in the GDP growth and add 0.4 percent to the annual U.S. workers' productivity growth over the next sixteen years. The expected growth of business use of the Internet has (not surprisingly) fueled the creation of companies aimed at providing services to current and future Internet users.

Most of the corporate mail is now transferred across e-mail. This system, as well as others, allows businesses to receive up-to-the-minute information about their competitors. Presently, the most common business use of the Internet is for communication.

Marketing on the Internet

One of the major advantages for businesses that use the Internet will be direct marketing. "You can just imagine the direct-mail crowd licking its lips at the prospect of the Internet: 20 million people who have sorted themselves into Internet groups from theologians to auto repair hobbyists. Better yet distributing junk mail electronically is lots cheaper than via snail mail—the U.S. Postal Service" (Tetzeli 1994). Marketing that uses technology to gain an edge with consumers will boom in the next five years, according to an exclusive *Advertising Age* survey. "As people get more comfortable with technology and realize the benefits of instantaneous communication, they will see the advantages and want to integrate that into their environment" (Spethmann 1993).

Marketers must begin the task of adjusting to the Internet to keep up with the activities of companies like Wal-Mart, K-Mart, and other leading retailers. Advertising is now done on the Internet. Publishers of electronic media acknowledge that just as in the print world, they will need advertising to subsidize their operations.

Globalization

Production and markets have become more globalized and integrated with the relaxation of trade and ownership barriers (e.g., NAFTA, the 1992 economic unification of Europe, and the current round of GATT negotiations), and through pursuit of aggressive growth targets by countries and companies (Wescott 1994). Furthermore, governments will allow new businesses to enter the market, which will produce surges in technology transfer.

Government and Global Networks

The U.S. Government, along with other nations, believes that the world has enough financial and technical resources to spin a global information infrastructure. The tremendous move toward the Information Age will bring about massive restructuring and transferring of technologies to the global infrastructure. If the Internet is marketed globally, it will require high standards of performance in quality, timeliness, total cost, and customer service. To reach these levels of performance simultaneously, it is necessary to change and improve "all" the phases in the value chain continuously.

"The White House and Congress are leading the aggressive move into technology transfer" (Hughes 1993). Most research into technology transfer of computer information has been developed through private industries with the help of the federal government. The research has been made possible by the Cooperative Research and Development Agreement (CRADA), which was developed in 1986 by the Federal Technology Transfer Act. The government plans to use CRADA to aid in the search for developing the global network.

Transferring Technology

The world is getting just a glance of the Internet. Before the real network is introduced, companies will transform or restructure their organizations to ensure success in the future. As the Information Age approaches, companies will stay focused on continual structuring by intertemporal technology transfer (Gaurud and Nayyar 1994). The development of the information superhighway will take a long time. During this time, technology will obviously change again. As technology changes, organizations will have to upgrade, as they are doing now, to compete. As technology improves, the market demand for it will increase. For instance, the Internet has existed for 20 years, but when the technology changed, it gave new life to the web. This change in technology brought demand for more products and services. However, the time lags involved in setting up the structure for consumers will be horrendous. "Information exchange and technology transfer foster the growth and development of new technologies, and the policies engendered by this approach to national security and defense have had a significant impact on technological growth, not only in the U.S. but also trading partners" (Mendelson 1992). Companies and countries are now examining the Internet to see how it will benefit their needs. "The role of technology has influenced in-house R&D expenditures in many companies" (Siddharthan 1992). Firms from around the globe are using the network for outsource services. It has given them greater flexibility, by providing quality services that the organization could not receive from their local markets.

Future of the Internet

The National Information Infrastructure (NII) believes that within 20 years current libraries and research tools will be obsolete (Messmer 1994). Newspaper publishing companies will likely be more powerful in the years to come because they can offer electronic magazines and up-to-the-minute information around the world. It is estimated that by 1999 almost $5 billion will be spent on network equipment, such as network interface devices and switches, and services to access modes (Rosenberg 1994). Businesses will become more service-oriented by offering many options to their customers over the Internet. Competition will become more fierce due to the rapid transmission of data. There will be more computer-related crimes from foreign and domestic businesses, and more hackers as well.

The Internet will bring customers fantastic games as well as important information. It will offer a larger variety of services that will be brought to citizens by the cable, power, and phone companies. The technology will bring new gadgets to the market. One example is a watch with telephone, television, and fax capabilities that allows a user to send and receive information.

Browser Wars

Netscape and Microsoft's Internet Explorer are the leading browsers on the Internet. These browsers convert electronic signals into readable web pages that have audio, visual, and interactive capabilities. Netscape began its marketing strategy by offering its beta versions free to the public. Thus, it has more than 65 percent of the consumer and commercial market share. Microsoft is not giving up. Recently, it began offering its updated version of Explorer 3.0 free to the public, with a view to capture Netscape customers, and it is winning the game.

CONCLUSION

The Internet is fascinating. It offers many services for consumers and businesses alike. One major advantage, besides rapid transmission of data, is that the Internet will spring new growth in technology. Such advances can produce positive changes (heart and lung machines) as well as negative ones (nuclear warheads). The information superhighway will link countries together to spark new development, especially for Third World countries. The Internet may also bring more of a standardized method for communication to the world. The Internet will open doors to many countries, and it could also cause political change in some nations. In China, people are using the Internet to express their feelings abroad. This is an advantage to the culture because they are not allowed to do so in their own country. In conclusion, the future of the Internet is immense and has important implications for high-tech marketers as well as consumers.

Appendix C: Just-in-Time Retailing

Allan C. Reddy

This chapter presents ideas related to the practice of Just-in-Time (JIT) in modern retailing in the United States. Most mass merchandisers and cooperatives formed by independent retailers claim to use JIT systems to reduce their inventory and overall marketing costs so that they can be competitive in the marketplace. With product life cycles getting shorter in high-tech markets (personal computers and camcorders, for example), retailers do not like to carry excess inventories that they can sell.

Just-in-time retailing is an American idea. Using JIT concepts in buying merchandise, mass merchandisers like Wal-Mart can maximize their profits while satisfying customers with low prices and quality merchandise. This chapter presents a glimpse of how JIT methods are used at Wal-Mart and discusses implications for other retailers in a high-tech era. It has three major objectives: to introduce JIT retailing as a concept; to show how JIT systems are used at Wal-Mart; and to present marketing implications for other retailers and direct marketers.

The JIT purchasing, inventory, and management concept was first developed in Japan at Toyota Motors to achieve manufacturing economies (Shingo 1982; ''The Export of Japanese Ideas'' 1987). Later, it caught the attention of U.S. manufacturers, who were concerned to cut inventory costs that reach as high as 35 percent of the inventory value (Berkowitz et al. 1992). They began using custom-built JIT systems (Frazier et al. 1988). General Motors, for example, could reduce $2 billion in inventory costs in one year by adopting JIT methods (Kotler 1991). Similarly, wholesalers, suppliers, and giant retailers, like Wal-Mart and JC Penney, are widely using JIT to increase their competitive position.

THE JIT CONCEPT

In manufacturing, JIT is basically a management philosophy whereby the primary objective is to achieve zero or minimum levels of inventory (Frazier et al. 1988). Manufacturers buy raw materials delivered "just-in-time" to be used in production, so that cash is not tied up in inventory. The benefits of JIT inventory management extend to traditional inventory management methods that rely on the economic order quantity (EOQ) model; this specifies the order size that reduces total costs of ordering and carrying inventory (Pride and Ferrell 1991). The benefits include elimination of waste, improved product quality, improved employee morale, and improved customer satisfaction (Inman 1991). Waste is reduced because the production goal is zero defects, which means less scrap and reworking. Product quality is improved for the same reason. Finally, employee morale is boosted because of fewer complaints from customers, who are more satisfied with products of high and consistent quality.

The principles behind the JIT philosophy are simple. Excessive inventory is quite expensive. As inventory levels are reduced, problems become obvious, and managers are compelled to solve them instead of ignoring them. Dealing with problems increases organizational efficiency, causing lower costs and improved customer service (Schonberger 1982).

JIT Retailing

Although it shares common background with JIT manufacturing, JIT retailing can be defined as the ability of a retailer to have just enough inventory for display and sales with minimum cash tied up in inventory. Also, in retailing, another name for JIT is Quick Response Inventory System (QR), which is a cooperative effort between retailers and their suppliers aimed at reducing inventory while providing a merchandise supply that meets customer-demand patterns (Evans and Berman 1992).

Today, because efficient buying of merchandise and maintaining of inventories at near zero levels are becoming critical to success, large retailers may have an advantage over smaller retailers. First, large retailers can negotiate more favorable terms from suppliers because of their large volume buying and long-term contracts.

Second, transportation and warehousing costs can be reduced by synchronizing delivery schedules with the retailer's merchandise needs and demand forecasts. Resultant savings can be passed on to customers via lower prices, making the firm's offerings more competitive.

Third, store shelves can be stocked with fresh merchandise because replacement orders are made at the point-of-purchase through electronic data exchange with suppliers, wholesalers, and manufacturers. This enables them to deliver goods at exactly the appropriate time.

Fourth, JIT systems enable retailers "zero customer feedback time." This means that as inventory moves through the system, retailers can find out which products are selling and which are not, and then delete the slow-moving items.

Requirements

The implementation of JIT system requires that certain conditions be met. Here are some important requirements:

Frequent and reliable delivery. This is critical to avoid an unnecessary inventory buildup. Suppliers must meet retailer delivery schedules or face penalties, such as being dropped as a supplier. Understandings and agreements must be negotiated with suppliers in advance, and to the satisfaction of both parties.

Communications link with suppliers. Retailers must establish electronic data interchange (EDI) with suppliers and their manufacturers and wholesalers so they can order merchandise directly from suppliers. Establishing these EDI links greatly simplifies and speeds up the reorder process and also helps increase sales, reduce markdowns, and reduce inventory carrying costs, by accelerating the flow of information and merchandise (Evans and Berman 1992).

Efficient coordination. It is important for suppliers to coordinate their delivery dates with retailer demand schedules, so that retailers can set up their merchandise displays based on delivery dates instead of placing rush orders, which are disruptive to both supplier and retailers.

Close relations with major suppliers. According to the "80/20 rule," eighty percent of purchases originate from twenty percent of suppliers. Consequently, it is important to maintain a close relationship with this group of suppliers.

Pitfalls

To achieve successful implementation, certain pitfalls must be avoided (Cunningham 1986; Karmarkar 1989):

Failure to obtain top management commitment. It is impossible to implement successful JIT systems in retailing without strong commitment and support from top management. Because it requires a total change in the way the firm operates, wholehearted support from management is crucial.

Inadequate employee education. Employees must thoroughly understand the concept, philosophy, and procedures of JIT. They must also be clear about their contributions and actions, which could decide the success or failure of JIT systems.

Failure to educate vendors. Not all vendors will show interest in a JIT system. It may not be advantageous to them because it may increase cost for them to satisfy buyers who demand deliveries "just-in-time." Therefore, an education program may be necessary to persuade new vendors to accept and participate in the firm's JIT system. One inducement here could be the guarantee of repeat orders and long-term contracts.

Failure to view JIT as an ongoing process. JIT retailing is not a cure-all for

Figure C.1
JIT Systems at Wal-Mart

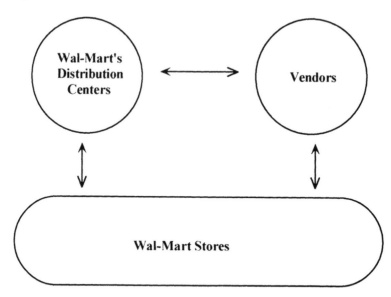

retailing problems. It is a concept that can improve competitive efficiency of a retailer. Nevertheless, any return on investment in JIT systems must be viewed over the long term rather than the short term because optimum results may not be realized until the system has been in place for some time.

Failure to design proper software. Coordinating delivery schedules with the firm's merchandise requirements is essential, and computer software that links with vendor computers is necessary to reduce delays and to improve accuracy.

Thus, firms considering adoption of JIT systems should first see whether they can meet the minimum conditions discussed above and avoid the pitfalls.

JIT Systems at Wal-Mart

Wal-Mart's retailing operations provide a good example of JIT retailing in practice. Figure C.1 shows the link between Wal-Mart's stores, distribution centers, and vendors. It is no accident that Wal-Mart's 1700 stores never seem to run out of merchandise, while the firm maintains inventories at near zero levels throughout its distribution network. It is an amazing feat in coordination— matching merchandise needs with physical distribution plans—considering the tremendous volume of business that Wal-Mart does.

At Wal-Mart, JIT systems are called "stockless systems." These systems are designed to reduce inventory levels because suppliers deliver merchandise according to mutually agreed-upon schedules. Employees that enthusiastically accept and make JIT work are rewarded through bonuses and recognitions, and suppliers that cooperate are awarded with lucrative orders and long-term commitments.

The "Retail Link" Program

Wal-Mart recently started the "Retail Link" program, which goes beyond the mere sharing of electronic data with suppliers. Under this program, vendors continually receive a variety of information on sales trends and inventory levels. They also receive purchase orders so that they can resupply merchandise on time. For example, a men's slacks manufacturer receives purchase orders directly via satellite links, enabling the firm to offer slacks in 64 sizes and various color combinations and to have them delivered promptly, even in peak seasons ("An Electronic Pipeline" 1987).

At store level, two types of purchase orders are used: warehouse orders and assembly orders. Warehouse orders constitute 80 percent of total orders placed by each store. These orders contain information such as merchandise item number, description, vendor name, stock number, unit costs, unit retail price, size, color, and markup. Merchandise is usually ordered by a hand-held electronic unit called Telzon, which can unload information to the mainframe computer at the distribution center.

About 20 percent of merchandise is ordered via assembly orders that go directly to vendors. In preparing these orders, a floor associate incorporates lead time, which is the number of weeks it takes for ordered merchandise to arrive at the store. Two factors are used in this calculation: a two-week safety stock and two four-week ordering intervals. The objective is to reduce unnecessary inventory buildups.

Two problems can occur with either of the above orders: stock-out or overstock. Stock-out happens when sales increase while order size remains the same. Because customers cannot get the merchandise they need, they usually patronize a competitor's store. Overstock occurs when excess inventory is accumulated, increasing a firm's carrying costs. Both situations must be avoided if the firm expects to remain competitive.

The Automated Inventory Replenishment System

Largely, Wal-Mart's success depends on its complex but efficient Automated Inventory Replenishment System (AIRS). The purpose of this system is to reduce managerial decisions to a minimum and ensure that the flow of merchandise throughout the distribution network occurs as smoothly as possible. This is accomplished through efficient computer linkages between the firm and its distribution centers and suppliers. Suppliers are continuously kept informed regarding merchandise needs.

The Distribution Center

The distribution center is the kingpin of AIRS and JIT retailing. By acting as a nerve center, it facilitates and ensures smooth flow of inventory from suppliers to distribution centers and from there to various Wal-Mart stores. According to CEO Sam Walton, the firm's rapid growth and profitability are due to its own version of "hub-and-spoke distribution" ("Wal-Mart Credits . . . " 1986). This is a system that enables management to take advantage of substantial quantity discounts in buying merchandise. Also, Wal-Mart first gives priority to location of the distribution center rather than location of the stores. This shows the importance that the firm gives to logistics and efficient distribution.

Each enormous distribution center is strategically established. For example, 205,000 cases of merchandise are unloaded daily at the rate of 132,400 cases per hour brought in by 190 trailers. On average, each center services about 150 stores within a 400-mile radius. Some eighteen distribution centers service more than 1700 retail outlets nationwide, and total storage space has grown from 11.8 million to 14.6 million square feet in a five-year period. Each distribution center carries about 8,000 items in stock worth $65.8 billion.

Annual inventory turnover rate is more than 15.8 times, resulting in $1.74 billion in annual sales. The 98.9 percent in-stock rate covers 99 percent of demand. Finally, if the system breaks down, idle-time cost is estimated to be about $127 per minute. The costs include fixed costs, overhead costs, and opportunity costs of probable loss of customers to competition. Therefore, it is important to keep the distribution centers working at peak performance levels without interruptions.

Besides its successful use of JIT systems, Wal-Mart has other major competitive advantages. These advantages include superior management skills, accurate sales forecasting, and use of appropriate technologies to operate its distribution network. Most important, Wal-Mart displays superior management skills in coordinating employees and vendors, who work in harmony to achieve common goals.

Implications

The addition of JIT systems may not benefit all retailers in the same manner. Some retailers may not have the inclination to take advantage of the systems. Wal-Mart's example illustrates how a retailer who uses the JIT system benefits from it by saving on inventory management costs.

Does a firm have to be as large as Wal-Mart to realize benefit from these JIT systems? There are no clear answers to these questions. Each retailer should decide whether shifting to full or semi-JIT systems is a worthwhile venture. Most small- and medium-sized retailers like to do business in traditional ways because flexibility is critical in such businesses as fashion merchandising and speciality retailing. This flexibility may not be possible under JIT systems because orders are received and handled in a systematic manner under JIT procedures. There is not much flexibility to make frequent changes.

Mass-discount merchandisers like Wal-Mart are driving many a retailer out of business because the latter are simply unable to compete with discount pricing. In fact, their inventory costs are usually high due to their inability to get quantity discounts and realize transportation economies.

Finally, small retailers have two options. First, they can form cooperatives to strengthen their bargaining power and receive favorable terms from suppliers. It is ideal for these cooperatives to possess and operate distribution centers as efficient as Wal-Mart.

Second, without adopting JIT systems, small retailers must consider adopting "positioning" and "niche marketing" strategies. Through these strategies, the retailer can fill gaps in the marketplace that Wal-Mart and other large retailers are unable to satisfy.

References

Adams, B. M., C. Lowry, and W. H. Woodall (1993). "Use (and Misuse) of False Alarm Probabilities in Control Chart Design." *Frontiers in Statistical Quality Control* vol. 11, no. 4, pp. 155–168.

Arlen, Jeffrey (1994). "Goody's: Facing the Future." *Discount Store News* vol. 33, no. 4 (February 21), pp. A18–A19.

Arnold, Edward, and Mathew Adlai-Gail (1996). "Pro Marketers Can Use Net to Continue Their Education." *Marketing News* vol. 30, no. 17 (August 12), p. 20.

Bates, Tony (1995). *Technology, Open Learning and Distance Education.* Hampshire, England: Routledge.

Bayne, Kim (1994). "Beware of Newcomers Selling Internet Expertise." *Business Marketing* (December), pp. 9–11.

Bearden, William, Richard Netemeyer, and Mary Mobley (1993). *Handbook of Marketing Scales: Multi-Item Measures for Marketing and Consumer Behavior Research.* Newbury Park, CA: Sage.

Benady, Alex (1993). "Trade Marketing Faces Challenge." *Marketing* (April 1), p. 8.

Berkowitz, Eric, Roger A. Kerin, Steven W. Hartley, and William Rudelius (1992). *Marketing.* 3rd ed. Homewood, IL: Richard D. Irwin.

Bernstein, Peter (1996). "Branded?" *Telephony* (March 4), p. 21.

Berry, Leonard L., and A. Parasuraman (1994). "Services Marketing Starts from Within." *Marketing Management* (January), pp. 24–36.

Binstock, S. L. (1981). "Americans Express Dissatisfaction with Quality of U.S. Goods." *Quality Progress* (January), p. 13.

Blackler, Frank, and Colin Brown (1985). "Evaluation and the Impact of Informational Technologies on People in Organizations." *Human Relations* vol. 38, no. 3, pp. 213–231.

Bradner, Scott (1996). "Is the Glass Nearly Full or Nearly Empty?" *Network World* vol. 13 (February 19), p. 17.

Brown, S. (1989). "Moderators and Mediators: A Review of Concepts and Usage in

Marketing Research." *Winter Educators' Proceedings, American Marketing Association*. Chicago: American Library Association, pp. 170–175.

Buckley, Tara (1995). "The Internet Shuffle: On-Line Service Marketers Are Racing to Provide Internet Access." *Brandweek* (March 20), pp. 34–36.

Buerger, David J. (1996). "Glee for Telecom Reform Gets a Dose of Hard-Headed Reality." *Network World* vol. 13 (February 12), p. 74.

Buskirk, Bruce D. (1986). "The Technology Life Cycle and Industrial Market Behavior." *Industrial Management and Data Systems* (November–December), pp. 66–82.

Buss, A. (1989). "Personality as Traits." *The American Psychologist* vol. 44, no. 3, pp. 1378–1388.

Callahan, Robert E. (1982). "Quality Circles: A Program for Productivity through Human Resources Development." In Sang M. Lee and Gary Schwendiman, eds., *Management by Japanese Systems*. New York: Praeger.

Champ, C. W., and W. H. Woodall (1987). "Exact Results for Shewhart Control Charts with Supplementary Runs Rules." *Technometrics* vol. 29, pp. 393–399.

Churchill, Gilbert A. (1979). "A Paradigm for Developing Better Measures of Marketing Constructs." *Journal of Marketing Research* vol. 16 (February), pp. 64–73.

Cleland, Kim (1995). "Marketers Brush off Hacker Attacks." *Advertising Age* (January 30), pp. 16–17.

Coombs, Gary (1996). "Keys to Creative Business Teaching via Distance Education." *Mid-American Journal of Business* vol. 11, no. 2 (Fall), pp. 68–72.

Coppett, John I., and William A. Staples (1993). "Telemarketing: The Dark Continent." *Journal of Marketing Theory and Practice* vol. 1, no. 3 (Summer), pp. 1–7.

Cravens, David W. (1996). *Strategic Marketing*. 5th ed. Burr Ridge, IL: Richard D. Irwin.

Crosby, Philip B. (1979). *Quality Is Free*. New York: McGraw-Hill.

Cunningham, William (1986). "Some Potential Problems in Just-in-Time Inventory Systems: An Initial Investigation." *Business Insights* (Fall), pp. 20–22.

Curhan, Ronald C., and Robert J. Kopp (1987). "Obtaining Retailer Support for Trade Deals." *Journal of Advertising Research* vol. 54 (December), p. 54.

Czinkota, Michael R., and Ilkka A. Ronkainen (1995). *International Marketing*. 4th ed. New York: Dryden Press.

Day, G. S., and D. B. Montgomery (1983). "Diagnosing the Experience Curve." *Journal of Marketing* vol. 47 (Spring), pp. 45–52.

de Bono, Edward (1996). *Six Thinking Hats*. Indianapolis, IN: NCCI.

Deloitte, Haskins and Sells (1982). *Forming R&D Partnerships*. New York: Praeger.

Deming, W. Edwards (1982). *Quality, Productivity, and Competitive Position*. Cambridge, MA: MIT Press.

DeToni, A., R. Filippini, and C. Forza (1994). "Manufacturing Strategy in Global Markets: An Operations Management Model." *International Journal of Operations & Production Management* vol. 12, no. 4, pp. 7–18.

Dhalla, N. K., and S. Yuseph (1976). "Forget the Product Life Cycle Concept!" *Harvard Business Review* (January–February), pp. 102–112.

"An Electronic Pipeline That's Changing the Way America Does Business" (1987). *Business Week* (August), p. 80.

Ellen, Pam Scholder, William O. Bearden, and Subash Sharma (1991). "Resistance to Technological Innovations: An Examination of the Role of Self-Efficacy and Performance Satisfaction." *Journal of the Academy of Marketing Science* vol. 19, no. 4 (Fall), pp. 297–307.

Elliot, John (1989). "BNR: Past, Present, and Future." *Telesis* vol. 16, no. 3, pp. 34–39.

Evans, Joel R., and Barry Berman (1992). *Marketing.* 5th ed. New York: Macmillan Publishing Company.

"The Export of Japanese Ideas" (1987). *The Economist* (April), pp. 34–35, 68.

Factor, Mallory (1985). "Wall Street Must Choose between Quality and the Fast Buck." *Wall Street Journal* (April 15), p. 18.

Feigenbaum, A. V. (1983). *Total Quality Control.* 3rd ed. New York: McGraw-Hill.

Fitzgerald, Kate (1995). "MCI Rings Up Gays via Direct Marketing." *Advertising Age* vol. 66 (June 5), p. 50.

Flynn, Leisa R., and Ronald E. Goldsmith (1993a). "Identifying Innovators in Consumer Service Markets." *The Service Industry Journal* vol. 13, no. 3 (July), pp. 97–109.

Flynn, Leisa R., and Ronald E. Goldsmith (1993b). "A Validation of the Goldsmith and Hofacker Innovativeness Scale." *Educational and Psychological Measurement* vol. 53, no. 2, pp. 1105–1116.

Foxall, Gordon, and Ronald Goldsmith (1988). "Personality and Consumer Research: Another Look." *Journal of the Market Research Society* vol. 30, no. 1, pp. 111–125.

Frazier, Gary L., and Raymond C. Rody (1991). "The Use of Influence Strategies in Interfirm Relationships in Industrial Product Channels." *Journal of Marketing* vol. 55 (January), pp. 52–69.

Frazier, Gary L., Robert E. Spekman, and Charles R. O'Neal (1988). "Just-in-Time Exchange Relationships in Industrial Markets." *Journal of Marketing* (October), pp. 52–67.

Fry, Andy (1995). "Scanning the Newsstand." *Marketing* (May 11), pp. 33–34.

Garvin, David A. (1988). *Managing Quality: The Strategic and Competitive Edge.* New York: The Free Press.

Gaski, John F. (1984). "The Theory of Power and Conflict in Channels of Distribution." *Journal of Marketing* vol. 48 (Summer), pp. 9–29.

Gatignon, Hubert, and Thomas S. Robertson (1985). "A Propositional Inventory for New Diffusion Research." *Journal of Consumer Research* vol. 11 (March), pp. 849–867.

Gatignon, Hubert, and Thomas S. Robertson (1989). "Technology Diffusion: An Empirical Test of Competitive Effects." *Journal of Marketing* vol. 53 (January), pp. 35–49.

Gaurud, R., and P. R. Nayyar (1994). "Transformative Capacity." *Strategic Management Journal* vol. 15, no. 5, pp. 365–385.

Ghemwat, Pankaj (1986). "Sustainable Advantage." *Harvard Business Review* vol. 86 (September–October), pp. 53–58.

Giges, Nancy (1988). "World's Product Parity Perception High." *Advertising Age* vol. 59 (June 20), pp. 66–68.

Girard, Kim (1996). "ATM Starts to Make Public Appearances." *Computerworld* vol. 30, no. 26 (June 24), pp. 55, 60.

Goldsmith, Ronald (1991). "The Validity of a Scale to Measure Global Innovativeness." *Journal of Applied Business Research* vol. 7 (Spring), pp. 89–97.

Goldsmith, Ronald, Jacqueline Eastman, and Jon Freiden (1995). "The Generality/Specificity Issue in Consumer Innovativeness Research." *Technovation* vol. 15, no. 10, pp. 601–612.

Goldsmith, Ronald, and Leisa R. Flynn (1992). "Identifying Innovators in Consumer Product Markets." *European Journal of Marketing* vol. 26, no. 12, pp. 42–55.

Goldsmith, Ronald, and Charles Hofacker (1991). "Measuring Consumer Innovativeness." *Journal of the Academy of Marketing Science* vol. 19 (Summer), pp. 209–221.

Goldsmith, Ronald E., and Leisa R. Flynn (1993–1994). "Opinion Leadership for Vacation Travel Services." *Advances in Business Studies* vol. 4, nos. 7–8, pp. 17–29.

Goldsmith, Ronald E., Leisa R. Flynn, and Jacqueline K. Eastman (1996). "Status Consumption and Fashion Behavior: An Exploratory Study." *Proceedings of the Association of Marketing Theory and Practice*, pp. 309–316.

Guy, Sandra (1996). "A Symbiotic Relationship." *Telephony* (February 19), p. 20.

Harasim, Linda (ed.) (1990). *Online Education: Perspectives on a New Environment.* New York: Praeger.

Harasim, Linda M. (ed.) (1993). *Global Networks: Computers and International Communications.* Cambridge, MA: MIT Press.

Harnac, Jo Ann, and Kathleen C. Brannen (1982). "The What, Where, and Whys of Quality Control Circles." In Sang M. Lee and Gary Schwendiman (eds.), *Management by Japanese Systems.* New York: Praeger, pp. 67–75.

Hayward, George (1981). "Innovation Centers in the USA." *Industrial & Commercial Training* vol. 13, no. 5 (May), pp. 158–161.

Hirschman, Elizabeth (1980). "Innovativeness, Novelty Seeking, and Consumer Creativity." *Journal of Consumer Research* vol. 7, no. 3, pp. 283–295.

Hughes, D. (1993). "Technology Transfer Now a Top Priority." *Aviation Week and Space Technology* vol. 139, no. 19 (November 8), pp. 40–42.

Hurt, H., K. Joseph, and C. Cook (1977). "Scales for the Measurement of Innovativeness." *Human Communication Research* vol. 4 (Fall), pp. 58–65.

Inman, Anthony (1991). "Just-in-Time: Alive and Well in the South." *The Southern Business and Economic Journal* (April), pp. 52–67.

Internet User (1996). Fall issue, p. 17.

Janah, Monua (1995). "I-way entrepreneurs." *Forbes* (February 27), pp. 90–94.

Johne, Frederick A. (1984). "Segmenting High-Technology Adopters." *Industrial Marketing Management* vol. 13, no. 2 (May), pp. 59–63.

Johnson, N. L. (1961). "A Simple Theoretical Approach to Cumulative Sum Control Charts." *Journal of the American Statistical Association* vol. 56, pp. 835–840.

Juran, Joseph M. (1993). "Why Quality Initiatives Fail." *Journal of Business Strategy* vol. 14 (July–August), pp. 35–38.

Juran, Joseph M. (ed.) (1974). *Quality Control Handbook.* 3rd ed. New York: McGraw-Hill.

Kami, Michael J. (1988). *Trigger Points: How to Make Decisions Three Times Faster, Innovate Smarter, and Beat Your Competition by Ten Percent (It Ain't Easy!).* New York: McGraw-Hill.

Kanter, Donald L. (1981). "It Could Be: Ad Trends Flowing from Europe to U.S." *Advertising Age* vol. 52 (February 9), pp. 49–52.

Karmarkar, Uday (1989). "Getting Control of Just-in-Time." *Harvard Business Review* (September–October), pp. 122–132.

Kassarjian, H. (1971). "Personality and Consumer Behavior: A Review." *Journal of Marketing Research* vol. 8 (November), pp. 409–418.

Kassarjian, H., and M. Sheffet (1981). "Personality and Consumer Behavior: An Update." In Harold H. Kassarjian and Tom Robertson (eds.), *Perspectives in Consumer Behavior*. Glenview, IL: Scott-Foresman, pp. 160–180.

Kelly, Keith J. (1995). "Publishers Pine for Cyber-Profits." *Advertising Age* (March 13), p. S-22.

Kohn, Carol A., and Jacob Jacoby (1973). "Operationally Defining the Consumer Innovator." *Proceedings of the American Psychological Association*, pp. 837–838.

Kotler, Philip (1991). *Marketing Management: Analysis, Planning, Implementation, and Control.* 7th ed. Englewood Cliffs, NJ: Prentice-Hall.

Kotler, Philip (1994). *Marketing Management: Analysis, Planning, Implementation, and Control.* 8th ed. Englewood Cliffs, NJ: Prentice-Hall.

Kottman, E. John (1977). "Promoting the Parity Product." *Journal of Consumer Affairs* vol. 11 (Summer), pp. 145–150.

Kuhn, Thomas (1962). *The Structure of Scientific Revolutions.* Chicago: University of Chicago Press.

Lauzon, Al (1990). *Enhancing Accessibility to Meaningful Learning Opportunities: A Pilot Project in Online Education at the University of Guelph.* Research in Distance Education (October).

Levitt, T. (1960). "Marketing Myopia." *Harvard Business Review* (July–August), pp. 45–56.

Levy, Michael, and Barton A. Weitz (1995). *Retailing Management.* 2nd ed. Chicago: Richard D. Irwin.

Lucas, J. M., and R. B. Crosier (1982). "Fast Initial Response for CUSUM Quality Control Systems." *Technometrics* vol. 24, no. 4, pp. 199–205.

"Managing High-Technology Portfolio Milks Cows, Kills Dogs" (1979). *Marketing News* vol. 13, no. 1 (July 13), p. 6.

Mason, R. (1994). *Using Communications Media in Open and Flexible Learning.* London: Kogan Page.

McCarty, Frank H. (1996). "Learning Faster and Better." *Manufacturing Engineering* vol. 117, no. 1 (July), p. 232.

McKenna, Regis (1991). "Marketing Is Everything." *Harvard Business Review* (January–February), p. 72.

Mendelson, L. D. (1992). "Technology Transfer Policy: Its Role as a Scientific and Technical Information Policy and Its Impact on Technological Growth." *Journal of the American Society for Information Science* vol. 43, no. 1, pp. 80–88.

Messmer, M. (1994). "Staffing the Information Super Highway." *Management Review* vol. 83, no. 11 (November), pp. 37–40.

Messmer, Ellen (1996). "Web Responds to New 'Indecency' Law." *Network World* vol. 13 (February 12), p. 9.

Midgley, D. (1977). *Innovation and New Product Marketing.* New York: John Wiley and Sons.

Midgley, D., and G. Dowling (1978). "Innovativeness: The Concept and Its Measurement." *Journal of Consumer Research* vol. 4 (March), pp. 229–242.

Miller, Cyndee (1994). "Top Marketers Take a Bolder Approach in Targeting Gays." *Marketing News* vol. 28 (July 4), pp. 1–2.

Miller, Cyndee (1995a). "Marketers Find It's Hip to Be in the Internet." *Marketing News* (February 27), p. 2.

Miller, Cyndee (1995b). "Retailers Do What They Must to Ring Up Sales." *Marketing News* vol. 29 (May 22), pp. 1–11.

Montgomery, D. C. (1991). *Introduction to Statistical Quality Control.* 2nd ed. New York: John Wiley and Sons.

Mulqueen, John T. (1996). "Users Can Celebrate Independence Day, Too." *Communications Week* vol. 59 (February 19), p. 62.

Muncy, James A. (1990). "Involvement and Perceived Brand Similarities and Differences: The Need for Process Oriented Models." *Advances in Consumer Research* vol. 17, pp. 144–148.

Muncy, James A. (1992). "The Production, Distribution, and Consumption of Sexually Explicit Material: Alternative Philosophies." *Journal of Public Policy and Marketing* vol. 11 (Fall), pp. 149–154.

Muncy, James A. (1996). "Measuring Perceived Brand Parity." *Advances in Consumer Research* vol. 22, forthcoming.

Narus, James A., and James C. Anderson (1986). "Industrial Distributor Selling: The Roles of Outside and Inside Sales." *Industrial Marketing Management* vol. 15, no. 2, pp. 60–69.

Nobis, Gianfranco (1993). "Trends and Integration in Food Processing." *International Journal of Contemporary Hospitality Management* vol. 5, no. 3, pp. 26–31.

O'Grady, Peter J. (1988). *Putting the Just-in-Time Philosophy into Practice.* New York: Nicholls Publishing Company.

O'Meare, Kristin (1995). "Book Your Vacation On-Line." *Travel Weekly* (January 30), pp. 15–16.

Pappalardo, Denise (1996). "FCC Sets Timetable for Reform Policies." *Telephony* vol. 9 (February 19), pp. 8, 10.

Peters, Tom (1987). *Thriving on Chaos.* New York: Harper & Row.

Poe, Richard (1995). *Wave 3: The New Era in Network Marketing.* Rocklin, CA: Prima Publishing Company.

Popper, E. T., and Bruce D. Buskirk (1990). "Growth Strategy for High-Tech Firms." Working paper, Bryant College, RI.

Pride, William M., and O. C. Ferrell (1991). *Marketing—Concepts and Strategies.* 7th ed. Boston: Houghton-Mifflin Company.

Pride, William M., and O. C. Ferrell (1995). *Marketing: Concepts and Strategies.* 9th ed. Boston: Houghton Mifflin Company.

"The Quality Imperative" (1991). *Business Week* (October 25), pp. 58–61.

Reddy, Allan C. (1994). *Total Quality Marketing: Strategies for Increasing Market Shares.* Westport, CT: Quorum Books.

Reddy, Allan C. (1996). *A Macro Perspective on Technology Transfer.* Westport, CT: Quorum Books.

Reddy, Allan C., and David P. Campbell (1994). *Marketing's Role in Economic Development.* Westport, CT: Quorum Books.

Reddy, Allan C., John E. Oliver, C. P. Rao, and A. L. Addington (1984). "A Macro Behavioral Model of the Japanese Economic Miracle." *Akron Business and Economic Review* (Spring), pp. 40–45.

Reed, David (1994). "The Turn of the Skew." *Marketing Week* vol. 15, no. 45 (January 28), pp. 33–34.

Reimer, Borge (1983). *Executive Vice President's Speech* (October 16). Canton, OH: Dana Corporation.

Rieker, W. S. (1977). *Quality Control Circles Study Guide*. Saratoga, CA: Internorth.

Roberts, S. W. (1959). "Control Chart Tests Based on Geometric Moving Averages." *Technometrics* vol. 1, no. 3, pp. 239–250.

Rockwell, Mark (1996). "The New Law: You Might Find You Get What You Need." *Communications Week* no. 598 (February 26), p. 42.

Rogers, Everett M. (1962). *Diffusion of Innovations*. New York: The Free Press.

Rogers, Everett M. (1983). *Diffusion of Innovations*. 3rd ed. New York: The Free Press.

Rogers, Everett M., and F. Floyd Shoemaker (1971). *Communication of Innovations*. New York: The Free Press.

Rohde, David, and Ellen Messmer (1996). "So What's in It for Me?" *Network World* vol. 13, no. 6, pp. 1, 14.

Roscitt, Rick, and Robert I. Parker (1988). "Direct Marketing to Consumers." *Journal of Consumer Marketing* vol. 5, no. 1 (Winter), pp. 5–14.

Rosenberg, R. (1994). "Your Electronic Future: At Home on the Network." *Telecommunications* vol. 28, no. 10 (October), pp. 46–47.

Rosenbloom, Bert (1991). *Marketing Channels: A Management View*. 5th ed. New York: Dryden Press.

Rosenbloom, Bert (1995). *Marketing Channels: A Management View*. 5th ed. New York: Dryden Press.

Ryans, J. K., and W. L. Shanklin (1984). "Ten Megatrends of High-Technology Market Behavior." *Business Marketing* (September), pp. 100–106.

Sambrook, Clare (1992). "The New Consumer Caution: The Miserable Life of the Careful Consumer—Staying in to Save Money." *Marketing* (September 17), pp. 19–21.

Schonberger, R. J. (1982). *Japanese Manufacturing Technique: Nine Hidden Lessons in Simplicity*. New York: The Free Press.

Shanklin, W. L. (1983). "Supply Side Marketing Can Restore Yankee Ingenuity." *Research Management* (May–June), pp. 20–25.

Shanklin, W. L., and J. K. Ryans (1984). *Marketing High-Technology*. Lexington, MA: Lexington Books.

Shanklin, William L. (1989). *Six Timeless Marketing Blunders*. Lexington, MA: Lexington Books.

Sherman, Stratford (1994). "Will the Information Superhighway Be the Death of Retailing?" *Fortune* (April 18), pp. 98–110.

Shingo, S. (1982). *The Toyota Production System*. Tokyo: Japanese Management Association.

Siddharthan, S. N. (1992). "Transaction Cost, Technology Transfer, and In-House R&D." *Journal of Economic Behavior and Organization* vol. 18, no. 2 (July), pp. 265–272,

Sloan, Pat (1989). "Battling Product, Ad Parity: Frost Urges Daring in Creative Agency Structure." *Advertising Age* vol. 60 (August 28), p. 47.

Smith, Peter et al. (eds.) (1991). *Distance Education and the Mainstream*. Hampshire, England: Routledge.

Smith, William C. (1992). "Nonwovens Industry Gears Up to Address Environmental Issues." *Textile World* vol. 142, no. 12 (December), pp. 67–68.

Solomon, Stephen D. (1994). "Staking a Claim on the Internet." *Technology* (November), pp. 87–92.

Spethmann, Betsy (1993). "William Morris Flexes Promotions Muscle." *Brandweek* vol. 34, no. 20 (May 17), pp. 1, 6.

Spethmann, B. (1993). "Markets Tap into Tech." *Advertising Age* vol. 6, no. 4 (January 25), pp. 30–31.

Stern, Louis W., and Adel I. El-Ansary (1992). *Marketing Channels*. 4th ed. Englewood Cliffs, NJ: Prentice-Hall.

Stern, Louis W., Adel I. El-Ansary, and Anne T. Coughlin (1996). *Marketing Channels*. 5th ed. Upper Saddle River, NJ: Prentice-Hall.

Struebing, Laura (1996). "Receive a QA Degree over the Internet." *Quality Progress* vol. 29, no. 5 (May), p. 15.

Taguchi, Genichi, and Don Clausing (1990). "Robust Quality." *Harvard Business Review* 68 (January–February), pp. 65–75.

Taylor, Cathy (1995). "Z Factor: Coors Brewing Company." *Adweek* (February 6), p. 6.

Taylor, Thayer C. (1987). "Computers in Sales and Marketing: S&MM's Survey Results." *Sales and Marketing Management* vol. 138 (May), pp. 52–53.

Tetzeli, R. (1994). "The Internet and Your Business." *Fortune* vol. 129, no. 5 (March 7), pp. 86–92.

"U.N. Report: MNCs Are Key to Growth of World Economy" (1993). *Crossborder Monitor* vol. 19 (August 18), p. 1.

U.S. Census Bureau (1992). *1992 Census of Wholesale Trade*. Washington, DC: U.S. Census Bureau.

"Wal-Mart Credits Deep Discounts to Hub and Spoke Planning" (1986). *Marketing News* (June 20), p. 10.

Walton, Sam M. (1986). *Annual Stockholders' Meeting*. Fayetteville: University of Arkansas.

Warner, Fara (1995). "Cheers! It's Happy Hour in Cyberspace." *Wall Street Journal* (March 15), p. B-5.

Webster, Nancy C. (1994). "Playing to Gay Segments Opens Doors to Marketers." *Advertising Age* vol. 66 (May 30), p. S-6.

Weinig, Sheldon (1990). "Oh, to Be Sold to the Japanese." *Across the Board* vol. 27, no. 5, pp. 34–38.

Wescott, W. F., II (1993). "A Quid Pro Quo for Transnational Corporations and Developing Countries." *The Columbia Journal of World Business* vol. 27, no. 9 (Fall–Winter), pp. 144–154.

Woodall, W. H., and B. M. Adams (1993). "The Statistical Design of CUSUM Charts." *Quality Engineering* vol. 5, no. 2, pp. 559–570.

Xin Li, and Nancy B. Crane (1993). *Electronic Style: A Guide to Citing Electronic Information*. Westport, CT: Meckler.

Xu, Gongli (1996). "Advantages and Disadvantages of Using E-mail as Instructional Aid: Some Random Thoughts." Adult Education Research Center, the University of British Columbia, Canada.

Zbar, Jeffrey D. (1995). "The Next Marketing Wave ... Doing Business on the Internet." *South Florida Business Journal* (February 17), p. 19A.

Author Index

Adams, B. M., 79
Addington, A. L., 64
Anderson, James C., 100

Barnette, Ron, 4, 25, 31, 153
Bates, Tony, 29
Bayne, Kim, 128
Bearden, William, 55, 60
Berkowitz, Eric, 137
Berman, Barry, 138, 139
Berry, Leonard L., 126
Bienstock, Carol, 4, 93, 153
Binstock, S. L., 66
Blackler, Frank, 55
Bradner, Scott, 48
Brannen, Kathleen C., 64
Brown, S., 55, 56
Buckley, Tara, 123, 128
Buskirk, Bruce D., 4, 7–8, 153
Buss, A., 56

Callahan, Robert E., 64
Champ, W., 79
Churchill, Gilbert A., 59
Cleland, Kim, 128
Cook, C., 58
Coppert, John L., 126
Curhan, Ronald C., 98
Czinkota, Michael R., 1

de Bono, Edward, 28, 30
Del Toni, A., 34
Deming, W. Edwards, 68
Dhalla, N. K., 9
Dowling, G., 56, 57, 59

Eastman, Jacqueline K., 4, 57, 153
El-Ansary, Adel, 95–96, 100–102
Ellen, Pam Scholder, 55, 60
Elliot, John, 55
Evans, Joel R., 138–139

Factor, Mallory, 67
Ferrell, O. C., 95–98, 138
Fiegenbaum, A. V., 72
Flynn, Leisa R., 55–57, 60–61
Frazier, Gary L., 100, 137
Freiden, Jon, 56

Garvin, David A., 67
Gaski, John F., 100
Gatington, Hubert, 59, 61
Ghemwat, Pankaj, 66
Giges, Nancy, 50
Goldsmith, Ronald, 55–62
Guy, Sandra, 49

Harasim, Linda, 29
Harnac, Jo Ann, 64

Hayward, George, 55
Hirschman, Elizabeth, 57
Hofacker, Charles, 55, 58–60, 62
Hughes, D., 134
Hurt, H., 58–59

Inman, Anthony, 138

Janah, Monua, 125
Johne, Frederick A., 56
Joseph, Jacob, 58–59
Juran, Joseph A., 68

Kami, Michael J., 67
Kassarjian, H., 56
Kelly, Keith J., 125, 126
Kohn, Carol A., 59
Kopp, Robert J., 98
Kotler, Philip, 95, 96, 97, 98
Kottman, E. John, 49
Kuhn, Thomas, 51

Levitt, Theodore, 23
Levy, Michael, 97, 101
Li, Xin, 30
Lucas, Leo, 40

Mason, R., 26
McGreak, Rory, 35
Mendelson, L. D., 122
Messmer, Ellen, 131
Messmer, M., 48, 49
Midgley, D., 56, 57, 59
Miller, Cyndee, 101, 123, 124
Mobely, Mary, 60
Montgomery, D. C., 73, 77
Mulqueen, John T., 49
Muncy, James A., 4, 43, 49, 153

Naurus, James A., 100
Netmeyer, Richard, 60

Oliver, John E., 64

Pagell, Ruth A., 4, 111, 153
Pappalardo, Denise, 44
Parasuraman, A., 126
Parker, Robert I., 55

Peraya, Daniel, 33
Peters, Tom, 66
Poe, Richard, 53
Popper, E. T., 8
Pride, William M., 95–98, 138

Rao, C. P., 64
Reddy, Allan C., 4, 7, 25, 64, 85, 154
Rieker, Borge, 64
Robertson, Thomas S., 59, 61
Rody, Raymond C., 100
Rogers, Everett M., 59
Rohde, David, 49
Ronkainen, Ilkka A., 1
Roscitt, Rick, 55
Rosenberg, R., 135
Rosenbloom, Bert, 95, 98, 100–101
Ryans, J. K., 14

Schonberger, R. J., 138
Shanklin, William L., 14, 65, 66
Sharma, Subash, 55, 60
Sheffet, M., 56
Sherman, Stratford, 102
Shingo, S., 126
Shoemaker, F. Floyd, 59
Siddarthan, S. N., 133
Smith, William C., 30
Solomon, Stephen D., 123
Spethman, B., 133
Stern, Louis W., 95
Superville, Claude R., 4, 63, 154

Taguchi, Genichi, 64
Taylor, Cathy, 55
Taylor, Thayer C., 126
Tezelis, R., 133

Vyas, Niren M., 4, 85, 154

Warmer, Fara, 126
Weitz, Barton A., 97, 101
Wesscot, W. F., 133
Woodall, W. H., 79

Yuspeh, S., 9

Zbar, Jeffrey D., 126

Subject Index

Actualizers, 97
APRANET, 129
Association of Internet Education (AIE), 40

Brand parity in the telecommunications industry, 49–51
Browser wars, 135
Business-to-business markets, 7

Cable Act of 1992, 47
Category killers, 101–102
Communications Act of 1933, 44
Communicators Decency Act (CDA), 4
Computer Conferencing System, 26
Consortium of Financing Higher Education (COFHE), 41
Consumers in the 2000s, 1
Cumulative Sum (CSUM) Control Chart, 77–78
"Cyberversity," 33

Distance education: as a complement to classroom learning, 42; as an integrated system, 38
Distance Learning Service (DLS), 41–42
Distribution channels: differences between merchant wholesalers and agent wholesalers, 100; environmental factors affecting, 95
Distribution channels of high-tech consumers: roles of retailing, 101–102; roles of wholesaling, 99–101
Doing business on the Internet, 123–124; disadvantages of, 125
Domain Specific Innovation (DSI) Scale, 60–62

E-mail instruction, advantages and disadvantages of, 12–14
Electronic learning, and disabled students, 34
Enterprise Computing Institute (ECI), 43
Environmentally Weighted Moving Average (EWMA) Control Chart, 83
Experience curve effects, 14

Factors impacting on distribution to high-tech consumers: distribution intensity considerations, 99; sociocultural factors, 95–98; technological factors, 98

General Agreement of Tariffs and Trade (GATT), 85
Generic products, 8
Global consumer, concept of, 85

Global lecture, 40
Global markets, 86
Global products, 8; and the role of multi-nationals, 86–87
Global university, 39–40
Government and global networks, 134

High-tech consumers: differences from regular consumers, 3; profile of, 2–3, 67; reasons for studying them, 2
High-tech education, 106
High-tech firms, cost of, 55
High-tech innovation, 106
High-tech marketing, 106
High-tech markets, 3–4
High-tech products: in education, 3; pro-moting, 108
High-tech warfare, 15
High technology, as a process, 55

Innovativeness: domain-specific measure of, 59–60; measures of, 58–59; model of, 56–57
Internet: advantages of, 29; advertising, 128; and direct marketing, 125; future of, 134; how it works, 128–129, 131; marketing, 133; security of, 127–128
Internet as a medium in delivering educa-tion using e-mail, 26–28; advantages, 29; disadvantages, 29–30
Internet society, 129–130
Intarnet marketing, 3–4

Just-in-Time (JIT): concept of, 138; pit-falls, 139–140; requirements, 139; re-tailing, 137–139; system at Wal-Mart, 140–142

Kanban system, 72

Living standards, worldwide, 88–91
Low-tech products, 8

"Made in U.S.A." label, 67
Magazine subscription system, 125–126
Mail order catalogs, 126–127
Manufacturers' sales offices, 100
Market segmentation, 15

Marketing management strategies, 109; distribution, 109; importance of, 105–107; pricing, 108–109; product, 107–108; promotion, 108
Multimedia Broadcasting System for the Third World, 38

National Science Foundation (NSA), 40
National Trade Data Bank (NTDB), 116–117
Niche marketing, 51–53
Niche strategies, 14–15
North American Free Trade Agreement (NAFTA), 85

Online collaboration project work, 27
Online group discussion, 27–28
Online help hot line, 27
Online material presentation, 27
Opinion leaders, 96
Oxford Academy, 42

Perception of falling quality in American products, 57
Philosophers in Cyberspace (PHICYBER): I, 32; II, 32
Philosophy courses via the Internet, 25
Poka-yoke, 64–65
Product Life Cycles (PLCs), 1, 7, 9, 107–108
Pure research, 9

Quality, and unsuccessful companies, 69–70
Quality circles, 63
Quality crisis, reasons for, 68–70
Quality experts: Crosby, 68; Deming, 68; Deming-Juran rivalry, 70–72; Feigen-baum, 72–73; Juran, 68–70

Reaching the high-tech consumer, 81
Reference groups, 96
Researching industry information elec-tronically: information sources, 111–115; using the Internet, 119–120

Shewart Control Chart, 73–77
Sociocultural factors, and demand for high-tech products, 95
State-of-the-art (SOTA) firms, 10
Statistical Quality Control, 73
Strivers, 97

Technological chauvinism, 16
Technology Life Cycle (TLC), 7–9; cutting edge stage, 9–10; mainstream stage, 16; market stake-out stage, 12–14; marketing variables throughout the TLC, 17–23; mature and decline stage, 16–17; state of the art (SOTA) stage, 10–11; uses of, 23
Technology Life Cycle, advanced stage

and market shakeout, 12–14; experience curve effects, 14–15; market segmentation, 15–16
Telecommunications Act (TCA) of 1934, 44
Telecommunications Act (TCA) of 1996, 43
Texas Instruments, segmentation strategy in niche marketing, 22

VALS and VALS2™, 97
Violence and obscenity, 48–49
Virtual classroom, 31–32

World trade, growth of, 85; environmental factors affecting, 95

About the Editor and Contributors

RON BARNETTE is Professor and Head of the Department of Philosophy at Valdosta State University. He is also a consultant for Microsoft Corporation. His expertise is distance learning and the use of the Internet in higher education.

CAROL C. BIENSTOCK is Assistant Professor of Marketing at Valdosta State University. She has published in various business journals. Her expertise is channels of distribution.

BRUCE D. BUSKIRK is Professor of Marketing and Assistant Dean of the School of Business at Pepperdine University. He has written several marketing textbooks and published articles in *Industrial Marketing Management* and other business journals. His expertise is marketing strategy.

JACQUELINE K. EASTMAN is Assistant Professor of Marketing at Valdosta State University. She is also Director of the MBA program. She has published in the *Journal of Business Ethics* and other business journals. Her expertise is consumer behavior and advertising.

JAMES A. MUNCY is Associate Professor of Marketing at Valdosta State University. He has published in *Journal of Marketing* and other business journals. His expertise is consumer behavior and sales management.

RUTH PAGELL is Director of the Emory University Library Center for Business Information in Atlanta, Georgia. She co-authored *International Business Information, How to Find It, How to Use It* (1994). Her expertise is information technologies.

ALLAN C. REDDY is Professor of Marketing at Valdosta State University. He has published several books and business articles. His expertise is marketing management strategy.

CLAUDE R. SUPERVILLE is Assistant Professor of Management at Valdosta State University. He has published in *Quality Progress* and other business journals. His expertise is quality control.

NIREN M. VYAS is Professor of Marketing and Acting Dean of the School of Business at the University of South Carolina at Aiken. He has published in the *Journal of Marketing* and other business journals. His expertise is international marketing.

ISBN 1-56720-072-9

9 781567 200720

HARDCOVER BAR CODE